VIOLENCE.
SPEED.
MOMENTUM.

VIOLENCE.
SPEED.
MOMENTUM.

DR DISRESPECT

GALLERY BOOKS

NEW YORK   LONDON   TORONTO   SYDNEY   NEW DELHI

G

Gallery Books
An Imprint of Simon & Schuster, Inc.
1230 Avenue of the Americas
New York, NY 10020

First Gallery Books hardcover edition March 2021

GALLERY BOOKS and colophon are registered
trademarks of Simon & Schuster, Inc.

For information about special discounts for bulk purchases,
please contact Simon & Schuster Special Sales at 1-866-506-1949
or business@simonandschuster.com.

The Simon & Schuster Speakers Bureau can bring authors
to your live event. For more information or to book an event,
contact the Simon & Schuster Speakers Bureau at 1-866-248-3049
or visit our website at www.simonspeakers.com.

Interior design by Michelle Marchese

Manufactured in the United States of America

10 9 8 7 6 5 4 3 2 1

Library of Congress Cataloging-in-Publication Data

Names: Disrespect, Dr, author.
Title: Violence. Speed. Momentum. / Dr Disrespect
Description: First Gallery Books Hardcover Edition. | New York : Gallery
  Books, [2021]
Identifiers: LCCN 2020044991 (print) | LCCN 2020044992 (ebook) | ISBN
  9781982153878 (Hardcover) | ISBN 9781982153892 (eBook)
Subjects: LCSH: Disrespect, Dr | Video gamers—United States—Biography.
Classification: LCC GV1469.3 .D57 2021 (print) | LCC GV1469.3 (ebook) |
  DDC 794.8092 [B]—dc23
LC record available at https://lccn.loc.gov/2020044991
LC ebook record available at https://lccn.loc.gov/2020044992

ISBN 978-1-9821-5387-8
ISBN 978-1-9821-5389-2 (ebook)

I dedicate this book to you, my dear readers.
Hahahaha. Totally kidding.
I dedicate this book to my mustache, Slick Daddy,
who's silky and masculine
and better looking than all of you put together.

I'LL NEVER WRITE THIS BOOK

Millions of people tell me every day that I should write a book about me.

"Help us, Dr Disrespect," they beg. "You're the only thing we care about in the universe. We won't read another *word* about anything until you write something about yourself. Please, please tell us the secrets of your lore. All we want is to truly understand you!"

I smile.

"I'm a six-foot-eight freak of nature with a thirty-seven-inch vertical leap, the Two-Time, Back-to-Back 1993–94 Blockbuster Video Game Champion, and the most dominant international gaming superstar in the history of the world," I say. "Truly understanding me is impossible. Now leave, before I smack you in the mouth with my flip phone."

They say, "Are you being serious right now?"

I say, "Maybe I am, maybe I'm not. Maybe I don't even know. Either way, I'm never telling you, you skinny punk kid."

At that point, the millions of people run for their lives.

But the joke's on them, because the Two-Time would never, *ever* do anything to hurt his flip phone. And the truth is, I already have dozens of books under my belt, including volumes 1, 3, 4, and 7 of the *Knight Rider* paperback series, which I wrote in my spare time under the nom de plume "Paul G. Fitzgerald." All *New York Times* bestsellers.

Of course, none of those books is strictly autobiographical, though the character Michael Knight and Jean-Claude Van Damme's actual personality were both loosely based on myself (lawsuits pending). And obviously the ravenous public is still desperate to know more about me.

So I wasn't surprised when some guy named Nigel called me up from Simon & Schuster wanting to meet about publishing an exclusive tell-all memoir. I even told him I'd take the meeting, not because I gave a crap what he had to say, but because it was a lunch meeting and I thought it'd be funny to order a lot of expensive shit on his tab.

I landed my jet-black Kamov Ka-27 attack chopper on the roof of the restaurant, this posh, exclusive club in midtown Manhattan Nigel recommended called App Lebeés, which I think is French or Swahili or something.

"Well, Nigel," I said as I eyed the restaurant's sumptuous neon lighting and inhaled the aroma of rich fried onions and meat, "if you're aiming to impress, you made a good start."

He stood. He was skinny, he was pasty, he was wearing tweed. I'll be honest—it felt a little on-the-nose for someone in the book biz to be wearing tweed. It's like, why not toss in a monocle and a bow tie while you're at it, you know? But whatever. So I started to give him one of my firm handshakes, but he and his fingers were so delicate and intellectual I was afraid I might crush them and miss out on my free lunch.

"Indeed," Nigel said nervously, "sorry about that, we had to cut back on our expenses—um, why are you wearing sunglasses inside?"

I snorted in contempt. My "sunglasses" were Google prototype scopes with built-in Sony 3D LCD technology and night vision, allowing me to scan even the darkest recesses of this dark, fancy restaurant for potential ambush by my thousands of enemies. But I didn't want to embarrass the dude, so instead I just said:

"I don't know. Why aren't *you* doing squats every day?"

"What?" he said.

I laughed and ordered the boneless wings, chicken wonton tacos, brewpub pretzels with beer cheese dip, and a double helping of Neighborhood Beef Nachos™.

"You, uh, must be hungry," he said.

"Nope," I answered.

"Doc," he started, then paused. "Hey—what *are* you a doctor of, exactly? I've always wanted to know."

"Right," I said. "You and everyone else on the planet. Now, what's up? My chopper is waiting."

"Doc, I'm going to level with you. We're in trouble. People just aren't reading anymore. Shakespeare, the Bible, the *Knight Rider* paperback series—we're publishing all the great classics, but no one cares. We need something fresh, something new, something electric to save literature. We need you, Doc."

I think he said something like that, but I don't know. I was too busy ordering the loaded chicken fajita plate with extra lime wedges, a full rack of double-glazed baby back ribs, and the double-crunch shrimp.

"Um, you going to eat all that?" Nigel said.

"Look, man," I said. "I've heard it all before. 'Blah, blah, Western civilization is nothing without you, Doc. Blah, blah, blah, you're the Chaucer, the James Patterson, and the Dolph Lundgren of gaming rolled into one.' I don't have time to save your pathetic humanities, okay? I'm too busy soaring with the eagles, I'm too busy climbing the mountain of success to the tippity-top, I'm too busy—"

I paused briefly to order the riblet platter, the eight-ounce top sirloin (extra bloody, because I knew it would gross out Nigel), the balsamic chicken apple salad (because I'm a beast but not a fucking monster), and the Triple Chocolate Meltdown® for dessert.

"Wait, where was I? Oh yeah. I'm too busy plunging down the waterslide of victory, all six-foot-eight inches of me Vaselined from head to tippy-tippy toe, with my bulletproof mullet dripping like black steel down my back, and my powerful mustache, a.k.a. Slick Daddy, a.k.a. the Ethiopian Poisonous Caterpillar, a.k.a.—"

"We'll give you a Lamborghini," Nigel said.

I casually took a bite of brisket quesadilla, which I didn't remember ordering, and which may have actually been Nigel's. It was delicious.

"First off, Nigel, I don't like being interrupted. Second, I obviously already own a 1990 Lamborghini Diablo, so . . ."

"I'm talking a 2021 Lamborghini Aventador SVJ."

I stopped chewing.

"Fine," I said. "I'm listening. What color?"

"Red."

I jumped up, sending chicken tenders and Bourbon Street shrimp wontons flying everywhere.

"Red! *Red?!* RED???!!! The Two-Time drives black, and black only!"

"But—but we already bought the car—I barely even have the money to cover this lunch!"

"I don't care!" I growled. "Take it back. Take it back or I won't save literature."

"Fine," he sighed.

"*And* I want a thirty-eight-foot offshore racing boat. *And* a matching trailer. *And* I want *that* connected to a 2021 Lamborghini Urus. All blacked out. *And* with an official Dr Disrespect Logo Decal™ on the side. But it's cool, I'll have my guy handle that last part. You can reimburse me."

So here I am, one day later, sitting in my multimillion-dollar state-of-the-art top-secret complex, surrounded by twenty doggie bags of leftover riblets and nachos, writing this book.

Nigel, who I guess is my editor or something—wait, are they allowed to change these solid-gold words? Is that even legal?—said something about finally sharing with the world the Doc's deepest, most intimate secrets. The untold history of my mysterious, legendary origins and my rise to unparalleled dominance. My treasured philosophies of life, victory, and wiping your ass while still sitting down. Grooming tips for how you too can achieve the perfect mullet-mustache combo (hint: you can't). And he really, really wants to know what, exactly, I'm a doctor of.

But let's be real here.

I'm gonna write whatever I want, and you and Nigel and the Champions Club and pretty much the whole world are gonna love it.

You really think I need his Lambos? I already own a warehouse full of 'em! You think I care about his racing boat? I have an entire fleet! You think I needed that free lunch from App Lebeés? I made a call on my flip phone twenty minutes ago and now I own the whole chain. (Turns out it's not French or very fancy, but I'm making them add an accent over the "e" just for the hell of it.)

I don't care what this contract says. This is *my* book. It'll have the rhythm of a sleazy seventies muscleman and the ruthlessness of a nineties serial killer. It'll fly with the falcons to a whole new galaxy of awesomeness. It'll stare down the long, dark alley of your fears and never look back.

So prepare yourself for a level of verbal domination never before experienced by man, woman, or child in the history of the written word.

Then again, no—there is no way to prepare. No way at all.

YAYAYAYA!

Yayayaya!

CHAPTER 1

MY MULTIDIMENSIONAL BIRTH

Every badass superhero has an origin story. Historians, scientists, and Nigel the Editor all say so.

Batman had that thing where his wealthy parents were murdered right in front of him in an alley when he was a kid. That must've sucked.

Superman had that thing where his whole planet was blown into a billion tiny pieces and his dying parents blasted him off into outer space. Also sucked.

Spider-Man got bitten by a radioactive spider. Actually kind of cool. But then his uncle got murdered by this dude Spidey failed to stop. Back to sucking.

But if it's not clear to you yet—just kidding, of course it is—the Two-Time is different. The Two-Time is special. So the Two-Time has not one but *three* origin stories.

One for each dimension I inhabit.

"But wait," you say, "why only three dimensions? Aren't there supposed to be more?"

You try kicking ass in more than three dimensions and see how great you do, okay? Being a multidimensional superstar is not easy, man.

"Hold on," you say, "how different is this really? Didn't you see that *Spider-Verse* movie?"

Shut up. If I say it's different, it's different.

"Wait, wait, wait—"

Hey! Whose fucking book is this, anyway? Nigel, you're supposed to be handling security here! I'm sick and tired of these interruptions!

So, as I was saying—three dimensions, three different origin stories. And here's the critical fact you need to understand: each of them is equally valid, okay? They're all completely true *and* completely false. Completely authentic *and* completely fictional. Completely silent, like the stealthy snake, *and* completely roaring, like the jungle cat. All at the same time.

Okay, fine. Maybe the second-dimension story is just a little better than the others . . .

NO.

That was a test, and you failed it.

All my origin stories are equal. All different, and all the same. Maybe that doesn't make any sense, but trust me—it does. Oh yes, it does.

Think about it.*

---

* Maybe you even heard of *another* origin story where I got my start in a small room with an old 1800s antique desk and a $300 Hewlett-Packard computer. Did it happen? Did it not happen? Is any of this *real*? OF COURSE IT IS. Every. Last. Word. Boom—that was just a fourth dimension. Yeah, try to keep up.

MY ORIGIN IN DIMENSION ONE

This will be hard, maybe even impossible, for your mind to comprehend, but in Dimension One there was a time when the Doctor wasn't the Doctor.

When I wasn't a chiseled six-foot-eight specimen of athletic superiority. When I didn't own a multimillion-dollar command center with its own helipad, and Slick Daddy was nothing but a dream above my trembling lip. When the Doctor didn't even have his master's degree.

That time was when I was ten.

The year was 1992. I was just a little tyke growing up on the mean streets of Oakland, California. Small for my age, skinny, my voice high-pitched and girlish. Cute face, of course, but with a shockingly weak jawline.

My parents were decent, caring people. My papa drove a minivan and sold used Chevys for a living, and my mama was a grade-school teacher who always wore a fanny pack. They taught me the value of integrity, honesty, and hard work.

But they didn't teach me any of the *important* stuff, you know? Stuff like video games, absolutely annihilating your opponent's will to live, or looking really, really good.

When I was even younger, like six, I'd begged them for a Commodore 64. *Begged.*

"Mama! Papa!" I squeaked. "We're talking high-impact Commodore prototype technology here. We're talking eight bits of processing, a full sixty-four kilobytes of RAM with a VIC-II graphics chip. We're talking *Arkanoid* and *Pitfall!* and *Contra* and more intensity than your minivan-driving, fanny-pack-wearing adult minds can possibly comprehend! I know I could be great at this! *I know!* Please please *pleeeeeeeeease* let me have one!"

That's right. Even as an emotionally repressed child, I had a flair for communication.

But shockingly, my parents refused. They wanted me to eat my breakfast and do my homework and read books. And not cool books, like this one, which might actually be the only cool book ever, and which obviously wasn't even written yet. But instead lame sissy books like *Little Women* and various dictionaries and almanacs, and other crap my editor, Nigel, probably read when he was growing up.

Most important of all, they taught me to always, *always* run from danger. I was too precious to them. They wanted to keep me safe, but instead of toughening me up, they taught me to hide. They taught me to run. They taught me to be afraid.

So my mind grew weak and my muscles became atrophied. I'd lie in my bed at night in my little book-themed pajamas, scared of the boogeyman, scared of the darkness that dwelled outside my safe little house, whimpering for my mama and papa, doing everything I could to live up to their expectations and follow their silly little rules.

So yeah. By the time I reached ten, I was getting my ass kicked pretty much nonstop.

Wild packs of eleven-year-old street punks would hunt me down after school, preying on my subpar reflexes and total lack of athleticism. They had rough-and-tumble names like Ramrod and One-Eyed John and Razor Frank and Steve, and they were armed with steel-plated Trapper Keepers and frozen Fruit Roll-Ups sharpened into shivs. Fifth graders can be tough little assholes in the East Bay.

I always ran. Always! Just like Mama and Papa said. But the punks would catch me in all my cuteness and innocence, and they'd hold me down and beat me to a quivering pulp. And I'd be crying and sobbing, this helpless, defenseless little ten-year-old boy, and—

—shit, hold on, I have to clear my masculine gravelly throat—

AHEM. AHHHHHHHEM-HEM.

—sorry, these are some hard-hitting First Dimensional memories. I'm getting fucking emotional here. Don't want any of my massive, superior tears to short-circuit this advanced experimental Dell Inspiron with twelfth-generation Intel® Core™ processor and WordPerfect 5.1 emulator I do all my word processing on—

AHEM!

—okay, cool—

And so then I'd whisper, "I don't understand . . . Why are you doing this to me?"

Then they'd laugh.

"Because you exist," they'd say. "And your body is puny and your voice is squeaky and your jaw is soft. And okay, we'll be honest, we're also totally jealous of the waterfall of glorious hair cascading down your shoulders. We wish we had hair like that, so we beat you."

Even at that age, my mullet was astonishing, and the Pert Plus 2-in-1 shampoo-and-conditioner I'd just started using left it supple and gleaming like black steel, so I couldn't really fault them on that one.

They'd finish bludgeoning me, and I'd scrape myself off the

pavement and limp home. My mom and dad would find me battered and bruised and bloody.

"Well," Mama and Papa would say, "just be satisfied knowing that you're the better person."

What . . .

A load . . .

Of BULLSHIT.

These punks were *kicking my ass*! Like, literally, this kid, I think it was Steve, he was always the meanest—he kicked me in the ass so hard this one time that his foot actually got wedged between my butt cheeks. Like it got *stuck* there for a solid three seconds. I thought I was gonna need the Jaws of Life to get this tool's Reebok out of my butt.

Shit still pisses me off. Even now.

Then one day, the pack of hoodlums came after me again. Again I ran.

But this time, as they were chasing me down the street, I saw an alleyway I'd never seen before. I ducked into it at the last second.

It was long, dark, and winding. So long, dark, and winding it felt like it would never, ever end, its shadows black and dripping and thick like tainted blood.

I could hear the gang of punks behind me, shouting, screaming, jeering. Getting closer and closer. So I kept running as fast as I could, till the air felt like fire in my little-boy lungs.

Then suddenly I tripped. I fell hard onto the pavement, the rough concrete cutting my palms and tearing a hole in my lame corduroy slacks.

I groaned and looked to see what I had tripped over.

It was an original Commodore 64, still unopened in its dusty old box. Somehow, for mystical reasons I couldn't yet fathom, the computer I'd always begged my parents for was lying here, in this random alley, among scraps of trash and rat turds.

Then, in my pain and delirium, I heard something in the distance. It wasn't the footsteps of my preadolescent tormentors. It was the sound of an eagle screaming its rage.

An eagle? *What the heck?*

(I was so damn innocent, "heck" was my go-to profanity.)

I looked up from the grime and filth. There in that dark, winding, endless Oakland alleyway, I saw the massive heights of Mount Olympus looming over me. A giant eagle circled the tippy-top of the snow-covered peak, flames in his eyes and danger in his heart. Just below him, a vicious, muscular lion clawed his way over the ice, roaring in anger and dominance. Just below him, a powerful green python slithered and squirmed, hot black venom dripping from his razor-sharp fangs. And just below him, an ancient Celtic warrior held the beating heart of his enemy up to the blazing sun right before he took a big, juicy bite, with blood and guts and veins spurting all over him and the pure, white, freshly fallen snow.

Yeah, it was a lot to take in.

Now, maybe my brain got jolted by my fall—but maybe, just maybe, it was a sign. A message. A calling to be something great, to be something bigger and better than what I was. And to kick the crap out of the little turds who kept bullying me.

I thought about it for a sec, shrugged, and chose the call to greatness and ass-kicking.

My attackers were on me in a flash. I leapt up, computer box in hand, and smashed Ramrod over the head, knocking him out cold. *Ugh!*

I quickly disarmed Razor Frank, who was only carrying a disposable Bic. *Shing!*

I spun around and caught One-Eyed John right in his pudgy loose gut. *Grunt!*

And finally, saving my best for last, I walloped that little shit Steve right in his ass. For a second I thought about wedging my foot there for payback, but I decided I was better than that, and I settled for spanking him like the little bitch he was. *Oof!*

The rest of the mob—there must've been at least nine more—saw my utter, unstoppable dominance, turned tail, and ran for their lives.

Lying in the dust, Steve looked up at me and squinted. "Who—who are you?"

Which was kinda weird, because we all went to the same school, and my mom was actually their teacher, so they really should've known my name, but it was a powerful moment and I was sick of my old weak identity anyway, so I just went with it. I chose a new name. A name forged in the flames of the sun, born in the cry of the hawk, and suckled on the sweet teat of Victory.

"The name is Dr Disrespect."

For some weird, supernatural reason, there was this amazing, badass reverb when I said it:

"The name-ame-ame is Doctor-octor-octor Disrespect-ect-ect-ect."

Steve frowned. "Why are you making that funny echo noise with your mouth?"

"Shut up," I said. "Or I really will shove this Commodore 64 up your butt."

At that very moment, I felt my jawline harden and square up, my voice grow deeper by 2.3 octaves, and the first young tendrils of Slick Daddy sprout on my upper lip. Shit, I think my mullet even grew another couple inches in the back.

The punks ran in fear. I picked up the mysterious, fateful Commodore 64 to take home as my mighty prize. And then some old fat dude stuck his head out a door in the alleyway and screamed at me.

"Yo, you gotta pay for that fucking thing!"

Turns out I'd fallen right outside a CompuLand loading dock, and my mystical miracle machine was just part of a big new shipment. Not really sure how I missed that, because there was a giant CompuLand sign right above the door, but whatever.

The old me would've apologized and begged forgiveness, but the new me just flipped him off and stole it. Which was doing him a favor anyway, because the box was a gory mess and he really should've been selling Super Nintendos or IBMs or something. I mean, it was 1992, for shit's sake.

Back home, I plugged the computer into our TV, this dusty old black-and-white RCA. I hooked up the joystick that I'd also stolen, and I turned it on.

As I started to play my very first game of *Contra*, I could feel the electricity running through my body. I could sense the spirit of the warrior twitching in my twitchy abdominals, and I could hear my destiny of greatness calling to me in the wind.

"Woooleee-woooo! Wooooddleeeeee-wooooooo! Woo-wooo!"

That's what destiny sounds like, man.

Immediately I dominated.

My parents watched in awe from the other room. Honestly, they were pretty good parents, even if they were baby-butt soft. They even bought me a Super Nintendo the next day, because seriously, it was 1992. And also because they'd finally started to guess what I already knew: that their son was meant for greatness. For a reign of supremacy unprecedented in modern gaming. For a garage full of Lamborghinis and a vertical leap of no less than thirty-seven inches.

The Doctor was born.

A Short Break

Anyone else feel psychically exhausted by the First Dimensional journey of my creation?

What I like to do, during these rare moments when I'm overcome by raw sentimentality, I like to kind of shake it off, you know? Let the vibrations of the experience work their way through my stunning six-foot-eight frame.

So right now, let's stand up together, okay? Get that lazy, flabby, book-reading ass of yours out of your chair and start hearing the *music*, all right? Yeah, that's it—a super-badass electronic beatbox just running through your brain.

Bump-tsshhh.

Bump-tsshhh-tsshhh.

Yeah, there it is.

Now let's add a sexy, smooth lyric. Just imagine this light, feathery whisper of a voice.

"They call him Doc!"

Oh yeah. There it is.

Now we're gonna move our bodies, exactly like this:

Turn that head to the left, to the left.

Now turn it to the right, to the right.

Now flick that mullet to the left, to the left.

Now flick it to the right, to the right.

Now thrust those hips to the left, to the left.

Now thrust them to the right, to the right.

Bump-tsshhh.

Bump-tsshhh-tsshhh.

"They call him Doc!"

Congratulations, you've been emotionally cleansed. You're welcome.

MY ORIGIN IN DIMENSION R

Why should Dimension One always be followed by Dimension Two? Trite conventions are for weaklings and runners-up.

My second origin took place in Dimension R, the coolest dimension of them all. In this dimension things started out very different than they did in the last one.

In this dimension, instead of small, I was big for my age. Instead of long luxurious hair, I had a crew cut. Instead of a cute face with a weak jaw, I had a strong jaw but I was ridiculously ugly because of my crew cut.

And I was a girl. And I had this big fighting robot spider I controlled telepathically. And I had a cartoon mallet I used to bonk bad guys on the head. And I called my enemies "turtle-slappers and biscuit-boxers." And my name was Spider-Man. Oh, *Spider-Verse* already did all that shit? All right, fine. Never mind this paragraph, then.

But all the other stuff is true, and I also lived in Sacramento, which in Northern California is pretty much the exact opposite of Oakland. And my dad was a teacher while my mom sold used Chevys. If that doesn't blow your mind, I can't fix stupid.

In this dimension, by the time I was ten I was already playing video games obsessively with my friends. Every day we'd swarm the local arcade, Pinball Pedro's, engulf it with our youthful energy and machismo, and claim every game as our own—*WWF WrestleFest*, *TMNT*, *Fatal Fury*, and never, ever *Michael Jackson's Moonwalker*, which was for pussies.

I completely dominated all the other children in my gang. Their names were Ramrod and One-Eyed John and Razor Frank and Steve. In this dimension, they were my boot-licking lackeys, and they were also all different ethnicities than their counterparts in Dimension One, like Razor Frank went from being Hui Chinese to being Zhuang Chinese. You kinda had to be there, but trust me, it was cool.

I never lost a single game, knew nothing of failure or the probably bitter taste of defeat. And I was a grade-A, expert shit-talker.

My specialty was getting in other kids' heads, setting up shop there, and just kind of fucking around. Like if I was playing Razor Frank in *WWF WrestleFest*, I'd be like, "Yo, Frank, how is it that I'm only ten and I'm already your daddy? Like, is that even biologically possible? Like, can my future sperm magically go back in time, impregnate your mom, and somehow make you my bitch of a son?"

The kids would laugh, and Razor Frank would say something in Zhuang, because I don't think he even knew English, and then I'd use Sgt. Slaughter to body-slam his ass.

So I was pretty much the best. But I could sense there was something more. A higher plane of dominance, a more electric arena of competition I hadn't yet tapped.

I found it in the back corner of Pinball Pedro's, where the grown-ups played *Street Fighter II* at the big-money table. These dudes were the real winners in town, you know? We're talking guys with ponytails and thumb rings. Men in their thirties who lived with their parents, couldn't hold a steady job, but held the top record on the arcade's *Ms. Pac-Man*. The fucking champions of the only arena I knew.

And the stakes? The stakes were massive. Not cash—cash was for suckers and for dudes who had cash. No, these guys played with the only real currency of value in Pinball Pedro's, these little orange paper prize tickets you could trade in for cool shit at the prize window. A couple tix would only get you a little plastic spider ring or some shit like that, but stack up enough and you could get some major high-tech hardware, like a Discman. Well, not a real Discman, I think it was a Sanyo or something, but still pretty badass.

I'd watch these balding giants of manhood from afar, my eyes wide in awe and envy as Blanka gnawed heads and Ryu threw *"Hadouken!!"* and giant stacks of prize tickets changed hands faster than a Chun-Li helicopter kick. I studied the moves, soaked up the knowledge, and something told me deep down that maybe, just maybe, I could compete with these titans who were old enough to (probably) have pubes.

But for the first time in my cocky young life, I didn't have the guts to try. Most important, I didn't have enough prize tickets to bet.

Until one day I saw them playing a *new game*, their cherished *Street Fighter II* pushed to the side like a bowl of soggy Mr. T cereal. This new game had a level of action that made *Street Fighter II* pale in comparison. A level of violence. Of speed. Of momentum.

This new game was *Mortal Kombat*.

Blood spattering, heads decapitating, spinal cords dripping, lightning blasts exploding, screams of agony and rage and "FIN-ISH HIM!" echoing everywhere! I'd never seen anything like it.

I had to play it. *Had to.* But how?

I pushed my way through the crowd of greasy goatees and black pleather jackets, elbowing fuckers out of my way until I finally grabbed a joystick for myself.

"Hey," someone shouted, "you got enough tickets, kid?"

I was about to lie my ass off, when suddenly the crowd parted and a man stepped out of the shadows. He was skinny and pale, with a scraggly little mustache. He might've been twenty-five or he might've been forty—he had one of those weird young-old faces. He eyed the mob around me, pulled out a switchblade, and flicked it open, revealing a gleaming black plastic comb. He ran it through his oily, thinning hair. It was impossible not to be impressed.

"I'll cover him."

He slammed down a fat wad of tickets. It was a crazy-huge bet. I mean, I could've bought, like, a brand-new solar calculator with that kind of paper!

So it was like, *fuck*, you know? The pressure was *on*, the buildup was just insane, I had *no idea* what was gonna happen. Suddenly all my shit-talking arrogance just drained out of my body. I totally choked up, my mouth got all dry and sandpapery, and I went straight-up silent. My hands were sweating like a muscleman prizefighter's, my adrenaline was coursing through my veins like a Lambo at full throttle, my heart was pounding like an ancient shaman's drum.

BOOM! BOOM! BOOM! **BOOM!**

So I gulped . . . Took the controls . . . Chose Raiden as my fighter because he reminded me of *Big Trouble in Little China* . . . So much anticipation . . . So much suspense . . . So much anxiety . . .

And then, yeah, I pretty much just lost.

And, you know, that was it.

Look, I really don't know what else to tell you. I lost, okay? Some old dude in sweatpants with a ponytail and two thumb rings picked Sub-Zero and he beat my ten-year-old butt. I'm not going to give you the play-by-play, because honestly it was pretty embarrassing and losing is not, like, part of my brand. I'm seriously already tired of writing about this stupid little story of me actually *losing* for the very first time in my Dimension R life.

Anyway, after I got totally destroyed by this random guy—and let's keep in mind I'd never even played this game before and I was just ten, all right?—the skinny switchblade-comb guy came over. Still feeling like shit and totally unlike myself, I started to apologize for losing his huge stack of tickets.

He cut me off almost immediately.

"Boy," he said, "I've been watching you . . . from the shadows."

His voice was rough and scratchy, like Splinter's in *TMNT*.

"Whoa—you mean like the creepy bike-store owner Mr. Horton watches Arnold and Dudley in that very special episode of *Diff'rent Strokes*?"

(And if you're too young to get that reference, LOOK IT UP. Lazy-ass Gen Z–ers.)

"No," he said. "Not like Mr. Horton, although that's a great reference. I've been watching you, and I've seen that you're not like others. You talk too much, it is true. But you do not run from the dark places. You seek out conflict. You crave battle. You have talent. You simply need a teacher to help you hone it.

"I offer myself, humbly, as that teacher."

He used the switchblade comb on his mustache, which was weird because it was really thin, ratty, and pubey, so the comb was just going through like three long gross hairs.

"Who—who are you?"

"I?" he said. "I am the owner of this fine pinball establishment. I lurk in the shadows, hiding, seeing all, waiting for a student like you. You may call me . . . 'Sensei.'"

Suddenly this big blond lady stuck her head out from behind the prize counter.

"*What the hell you say, Billy?*" she shouted.

Sensei Billy rolled his eyes.

"Fine," he said, his voice no longer rough or scratchy. "My mom owns the place. But I run it for her."

"*Say what?*" she yelled.

"I help her."

"*My ass!*"

"Okay, so I just kind of hang out and play video games. But I'm very, very good at video games."

"*Get a job and a haircut!*"

He snapped the switchblade comb shut like a boss.

"I must warn you," he continued. "The training will be vicious. It will challenge your mind, punish your body, perhaps even shatter your very soul. You may actually die."

I shrugged. "Sure, why not?"

"Cool," he said. "So you, uh, want to set, like, a time to meet or something? I'm pretty much always free."

"Nah, that's okay," I said, heading for the door. "But I'll probably see you around or whatever."

"Great!" he called as it shut behind me. "Well, I'm mostly just here, so, you know—"

I didn't actually hear the end of his sentence because I was already gone. It probably wasn't important.

But then, over the next few weeks, my life turned into this kick-ass training montage straight out of *Rocky IV*, except I was both Rocky *and* Drago at the same time. And this was totally, absolutely real:

- Out of nowhere all of a sudden, that awesome Joe Esposito song "You're the Best" from *The Karate Kid* started blasting everywhere.
- Sensei Billy told me to mop the floor. I asked him if that would teach me some kind of cool muscle memory, and he told me his mom made him do it so he figured he'd make me do it. I told him to fuck off.
- Sensei Billy shouted, "Again! *Again!*" for no reason.
- I ran around the block a couple times while Sensei Billy smoked a clove.
- Sensei Billy brought out an old Casio synthesizer and made me play arpeggios to enhance my finger speed and agility, using both hands, starting at middle C and going faster and faster. I'd never played before, but I was like this natural virtuoso. Notes of fragrant sonic honey rained forth from my fingertips. Small children passing by began to weep. I finished the exercise, smashed the Casio to the ground, and never played again. I was just *too good* for this broken world.

- Just kidding, I sucked. I shouted, "What the hell does this have to do with *Mortal Kombat*?!," smashed the Casio to the ground, and never played again.
- I told Sensei Billy that if we didn't start actually playing *Mortal Kombat* immediately, I was gonna fucking leave and never come back.
- Sensei Billy agreed, then pressed stop on his Sanyo boom box. "You're the Best" stopped playing, and Sensei Billy muttered, "Goddamn song was driving me nuts anyway."

So yeah, it was all pretty frustrating and I lost respect for him almost immediately. But it did help me get my confidence back, because I was like, "I'm way cooler than this idiot, and I'm only ten." After all that garbage, he finally started teaching me about *Mortal Kombat*.

"Let me guess," Sensei Billy said. "You chose Raiden because he reminded you of *Big Trouble in Little China*."

"Duh."

"You have good taste in movies, but that was a mistake. He's a split second slower than other characters, and he has a tell whenever he performs his flying-torpedo move. It's lightning fast—haha, see what I did there?—but he crouches *right before* he takes off. A good player will see this, block the move, and effectively counterattack before you can recover."

I thought about it for a second. Finally there was nothing I could do but admit it.

"Shit," I said, "you said something that makes sense."

"Thank you," he said. "The optimal fighter to choose is Sub-Zero. He's as quick as anyone, his recovery time is fast, so you can flow from one move to another almost seamlessly, and if you time his slide attack right, you can 'juggle' your blows—hitting your opponent with a combination of punches and kicks while he's still stunned. Cheap, but effective. And his ice blast is faster than the spear throw of Scorpion, his duplicate. Plus, everyone knows blue is cooler than yellow."

"Okay, you're gonna have to stop, because I'm just *that* shocked you're not a total moron."

He ran the switchblade comb through his hair. "Talk, talk, talk," he said. "Your talk is worthless! All that matters is victory. Come, we play!"

He got his mom to let us practice after the arcade's normal hours. I guess that was pretty cool, but I still wouldn't mop his damn floor. Instead he tutored me as I played Sub-Zero versus the computer, over and over again. I mastered the timing of Sub-Zero's every move, his ice blast and his sliding kick—I mean, honestly, he only had two special moves in the very first *Mortal Kombat*, so that part wasn't super hard. I gained patience in executing each block and punch and kick, learning not to overload the game with my incredible speed. And I perfected his glorious fatality, tearing the skull and the wriggly-squiggly spinal cord from one opponent after another.

Finally, after at least one hour of more or less pretty consistent practice . . .

"Holy shit!" I said. "I don't know about you, Sensei Billy, but I'm really, really impressed with myself. Like, I am good on a *cosmic* level. Probably the best. Definitely better than you. I think I'm ready for some prime-time competition."

"No!" he shouted. "Your skill is good, yes. Your speed is good, yes. But you still talk too much! And it's not even cute in a 'preco-cious little child' way! It's just annoying! You're not ready!"

"Nah, I'm totally ready."

He sighed.

"Whatever."

The next day after school I got to Pinball Pedro's and went straight back to that sweaty corner of champions. His face grim, Sensei Billy put down a stack of prize tickets even bigger than the first one—absolutely huge, enough to buy one of those shoe-phones you got with a subscription to *Sports Illustrated*. A crowd gathered around, all my bros were there—it felt like the whole arcade was watching, waiting to see the little ten-year-old get humiliated yet again.

But unlike last time, I didn't even sweat it. Unlike last time, I barely even cared. I knew I would dominate. And that's exactly what I did.

With Sub-Zero as my fighter, I tore through one so-called op-ponent after another: Liu Kangs, Sonya Blades, other Sub-Zeros, it didn't even matter. I'd knock 'em sky-high with an uppercut, get them with a slide move before they could even hit the ground, then attack again before they had a chance to recover. I was fucking relentless. And I'd finish them off with spine rips that somehow felt more bloody, more violent, and more triumphant with every single fatality. With each kill a new ponytail went limp, another pudgy tummy quaked with fear, another grown man went crying back to his mommy—which was easy, because they all still lived with their parents.

And I? I grew a little taller with each win, my voice got a little deeper, my hair grew a little longer, my face became a little more chiseled. My stack of tickets grew bigger and bigger.

Finally it was over. Or at least that was what Sensei Billy thought.

"Well done, my young grasshopper," he said. "You now have more prize tickets than anyone in history. You can finally buy a Sanyo Personal Compact Disc Player. Your victory is complete."

I smiled. And damn, I looked good.

"But it's *not* complete," I said. "I still have one more opponent to destroy." I pointed right at him. Just in case it still wasn't clear, I whispered the word "You."

"What!" he shouted. "You dare challenge me in my own dojo?"

"It's your mother's."

"Nonetheless," he said. "You dare?!"

"Yes," I said. "I'm grateful for the training you gave me, especially once you stopped trying to make me mop the floor. But you and I both know there can only be one champion. We will fight not for prize tickets, and not even for honor, because I honestly don't think you have any."

"Fair."

"No, we will fight for . . . your switchblade comb."

The crowd gasped. My old crew was basically shitting themselves. Razor Frank said something in Zhuang and I thought, "I really need to learn some Zhuang one of these days." Even Sensei Billy's mom was all fired up—she started passing out free Cokes and Sunny D to everyone. She was sick of her son's lazy ass.

"Fine," Sensei Billy said. "Yet again, you talk too much. This time, it will be your undoing."

"Nah," I said. "Because I understand something you never will. Winning isn't just about timing or speed or technique . . ."

I put in a quarter to start a new game, scrolled past Sub-Zero, and chose my fighter—*Raiden.*

"It's about being really, really good at talking shit."

His eyes flashed in anger, and just like that, I was in the dude's head.

Round one of the best-out-of-three match began, and the action was more intense than anything I, or probably any elite warrior in the history of mankind, had experienced before. He chose Sub-Zero as his fighter, of course. And although it was a pretty badass move for me to select Raiden, that limited me to simple punches and kicks and blocks, because Sensei Billy and I both knew the tell to my special flying-torpedo move. If I even tried it, he'd just block me and beat my ass.

Plus—and I hate to admit this—the dude was fucking good. His reflexes, his tactics, his kinetics were all off the charts. Nothing seemed to rattle him. He was totally locked in. Pure focus, pure concentration. Pure silence.

And that was my in.

"Are you really gonna do that? Like, that's your actual move right now?"

He was right in the middle of a combo attack—actually pretty nice—but out of the corner of my eye I saw him flinch.

"Shit, so damn predictable!" I shouted. "Look, look, look—I bet I know what you're gonna do now, I can totally read your mind, you're gonna do an ice blast . . . *now!*"

I mean, Sub-Zero only had two special moves, the slide and the ice blast, so it wasn't exactly brain surgery—but that didn't matter right now.

"You did it!" I howled. "YOU DID IT! See, I knew you were gonna do it. I knew it! I can read your mind, dude!"

His hand slipped on the joystick, and I got in a combo attack of my own.

"I saw that!" I said. "Your fucking hands are sweating!"

"Hey, watch the language!" his mom shouted from the back.

"Sorry, Mrs. C!" I called.

Then to him: "Honestly, I have no idea what your mom's name is, but I was feeling 'Mrs. C' so I just went with it. Hey, does that stringy thin mustache of yours just *look* like pubes, or did you actually have that, like, surgically transplanted from your nether region?"

This guy got so annoyed, he actually reached up to check his damn mustache—and at that moment I caught him with an uppercut that sent him flying, blood spurting and spraying everywhere.

"FINISH HIM!" the announcer commanded.

And that's what I did.

I'd won the first round, but I still had to win another to get best out of three. And then, yeah, I went and lost round two.

Don't ask for details. There's nothing interesting about losing.

"I meant to lose that one," I said, smirking. "Seriously, I totally did. I just did it to mess with ya."

And you know what? I said it so seriously, with such amazing, ridiculous confidence, with such massive, gigantic ten-year-old balls, that somewhere deep down I could tell he believed me. Shit, I almost believed myself.

"More speed! More violence! More intensity! More momentum!" I bellowed.

Round three had started, and now I was just yelling stuff because I liked the way it felt.

"More RPM! More revolutions per minute! Per mullet! Per majesty! Pure SPEEEEEEEED!"

People were starting to worry about my sanity. But fuck it, this was the new me—and it was working. I thought Sensei Billy's eyeballs just might pop out of his pimply head.

"MORE MORE MORE MORE MORE!" I demanded.

And then, right when he was most distracted, right when he was most confused, right when he was about to diarrhea in his sweatpants, I took my shot. I unleashed Raiden's flying-torpedo move.

"*Wajeee wajaa jayyyyy!*" Raiden screamed as he shot through the air.

(Some claim he's saying "Your mother's from LA!" or "Get back in the car!" Others say it's Japanese. But they're all idiots and I'm right.)

Sensei Billy tried desperately to block me—but he was a tenth of a second too late.

Raiden slammed into Sub-Zero, smashing him into the wall. Sub-Zero stumbled, dizzy, and I hit him with the flying torpedo again and again.

"FINISH HIM!" the announcer commanded.

But this very last time, I held back. I decided not to use Raiden's fatality, because I'm a gracious opponent and classy sportsman.

Totally kidding!

I blasted Sub-Zero's head into a billion little pieces, reached my hands up to the sky, and shot lighting at the gods with a final mighty shout.

"Fuck," Sensei Billy said.

"Talk, talk, talk," I said. "All that matters is victory." It was ironic because of before.

The crowd cheered, obviously. They wanted to lift me on their shoulders but I didn't think it would look cool. Sensei Billy sighed, ran his switchblade comb through his dirty hair one last time, and handed it to me.

"You were the son I never had," he said. "Or at least the son I shouldn't have until I can support myself financially. Now go and never come back."

I took the comb, shrugged, and turned to leave. I was done with this place. I had bigger, better things to dominate.

"Wait!" he said. "I never did get your name."

"Really?" I said, stopping. "After all this time?"

"Kinda weird, right?" he said.

"The name," I said, "is Dr Disrespect."

For some weird, supernatural reason there was this amazing, badass reverb when I said it. So it sounded like:

"The name-ame-ame is Doctor-octor-octor Disrespect-ect-ect ect."

"Cool echo noise," Sensei Billy said.

"I know," I said.

I gave him a firm handshake. When all was said and done, he had been a worthy competitor.

Then I went home and immediately washed that damn comb— like literally boiled it in Mr. Clean—because, man, his hair was filthy. It's the same switchblade comb I use to this day. At least in Dimension R.

And just like that, the Doctor was born.

MY ORIGIN IN DIMENSION #;K@1}`

So yeah, my Dimension #;K@1}` origin is pretty simple, all right?

I was born on this dying alien planet, and my parents launched me into space right before the whole place exploded. Then I landed on Earth and was adopted by these really, really rich parents who were both killed by these robbers in a dark alley after the opera, then I got bit by a radioactive spider, then my uncle got murdered by another robber when I was giving pro wrestling a try. Then I went to this secret island called Themychlamydia, where I was the daughter of Hippolyta with a cool prototype lasso, and I had the violence of Athena and the speed of Aphrodite and the momentum of Hera, and then I got this green power ring from some alien dude. Oh yeah, and I could talk to fish and I was all ripped and muscly and Hawaiian and spoke fluent Dothraki.

Then I was like:

"The name is Dr Disrespect."

Except for some weird, supernatural reason that I totally couldn't guess or understand, it had this badass reverb when I said it. So it sounded like:

"The name-ame-ame is Doctor-octor-octor Disrespect-ect-ect-ect."

And with that, the Doctor was born.

CHAPTER 2

LET'S SET A RECORD, BABY!

Did you think this was gonna be one of those stupid old-school books where you just sit around and do passive things like "read words" and "be entertained"?

Because if you did, you should probably just close this book and go back to your simple sheeplike life of grazing the tasty fields of mediocrity right now.

On second thought, I don't want you returning the book for a refund. I mean, let's not get crazy here.

But you should know that what we're about to embark on together will demand a higher level of excellence and dominance and stone-cold-killer ruthlessness than you, dear reader, have ever experienced.

That's right, we're about to break a world record.

And not just any world record. We're talking about possibly the oldest, most sacred record ever established in the annals of history: the record for the most people screaming my custom, legally trade-marked Dr Disrespect Battle Cry™ "yayaya" at one time, across the Earth, for at least a minute and a half.

Now, I know what you're thinking.

You're thinking, "Doc, but I just checked the *Guinness Book of World Records*, and I don't see any record listed for the number of people screaming your custom Dr Disrespect Battle Cry™ 'yayaya' at one time, across the Earth, for at least a minute and a half, or actually anything that even, like, sounds like that at all."

And my answer is that *making history* has nothing to do with small-minded *facts* and everything to do with *greatness*.

Also, you're looking at the wrong edition of the *Guinness Book of World Records*. There was a special edition released in Japan in 1972, and it very specifically states that the record for the number of people screaming my Dr Disrespect Battle Cry™ "yayaya" at one time, across the Earth, for at least a minute and a half, was set in March of that year with 1,322,417 people. It's a really rare book, like a collector's item, and I'm lucky I found a copy.

Cool, so here's what we're gonna do. At the count of three, we're all gonna start screaming the "yayaya"s. I'll type them out for you on my prototype Dell Inspiron with WordPerfect 5.1 emulator. And make sure you read every last "ya," because I'm timing it perfectly to get to one minute and thirty seconds.

All right, ready? Okay, one-two-three-**go!**

Yayayayayayayayayayayayayayayayayayayayayayayayayayaya
yayayayayayayayayayayayayayayayayayayayayayayayayayaya
yayayayayayayayayayayayayayayayayayayayayayayayayayaya
yayayayayayayayayayayayayayayayayayayayayayayayayayaya
yayayayayayayayayayayayayayayayayayayayayayayayayayaya
yayayayayayayayayayayayayayayayayayayayayayayayayayaya
yayayayayayayayayayayayayayayayayayayayayayayayayayaya
yayayayayayayayayayayayayayayayayayayayayayayayayayaya

yayayayayayayayayayayayayayayayayayayayayayayayayayayaya
yayayayayayayayayayayayayayayayayayayayayayayayayayayaya
yayayayayayayayayayayayayayayayayayayayayayayayayayayaya
yayayayayayayayayayayayayayayayayayayayayayayayayayayaya
yayayayayayayayayayayayayayayayayayayayayayayayayayayaya
yayayayayayayayayayayayayayayayayayayayayayayayayayayaya
yayayayayayayayayayayayayayayayayayayayayayayayayayayaya
yayayayayayayayayayayayayayayayayayayayayayayayayayayaya
yayayayayayayayayayayayayayayayayayayayayayayayayayayaya
yayayayayayayayayayayayayayayayayayayayayayayayayayayaya
yayayayayayayayayayayayayayayayayayayayayayayayayayayaya
yayayayayayayayayayayayayayayayayayayayayayayayayayayaya
yayayayayayayayayayayayayayayayayayayayayayayayayayayaya
yayayayayayayayayayayayayayayayayayayayayayayayayayayaya
yayayayayayayayayayayayayayayayayayayayayayayayayayayaya
yayayayayayayayayayayayayayayayayayayayayayayayayayayaya
yayayayayayayayayayayayayayayayayayayayayayayayayayayaya
yayayayayayayayayayayayayayayayayayayayayayayayayayayaya
yayayayayayayayayayayayayayayayayayayayayayayayayayayaya
yayayayayayayayayayayayayayayayayayayayayayayayayayayaya
yayayayayayayayayayayayayayayayayayayayayayayayayayayaya
yayayayayayayayayayayayayayayayayayayayayayayayayayayaya
yayayayayayayayayayayayayayayayayayayayayayayayayayayaya
yayayayayayayayayayayayayayayayayayayayayayayayayayayaya
yayayayayayayayayayayayayayayayayayayayayayayayayayayaya
yayayayayayayayayayayayayayayayayayayayayayayayayayayaya
yayayayayayayayayayayayayayayayayayayayayayayayayayayaya
yayayayayayayayayayayayayayayayayayayayayayayayayayayaya

yayayayayayayayayayayayayayayayayayayayayayayayayayayaya
yayayayayayayayayayayayayayayayayayayayayayayayayayayaya
yayayayayayayayayayayayayayayayayayayayayayayayayayayaya
yayayayayayayayayayayayayayayayayayayayayayayayayayayaya
yayayayayayayayayayayayayayayayayayayayayayayayayayayaya
yayayayayayayayayayayayayayayayayayayayayayayayayayayaya
yayayayayayayayayayayayayayayayayayayayayayayayayayayaya
yayayayayayayayayayayayayayayayayayayayayayayayayayayaya
yayayayayayayayayayayayayayayayayayayayayayayayayayayaya
yayayayayayayayayayayayayayayayayayayayayayayayayayayaya
yayayayayayayayayayayayayayayayayayayayayayayayayayayaya
yayayayayayayayayayayayayayayayayayayayayayayayayayayaya
yayayayayayayayayayayayayayayayayayayayayayayayayayayaya
yayayayayayayayayayayayayayayayayayayayayayayayayayayaya
yayayayayayayayayayayayayayayayayayayayayayayayayayayaya
yayayayayayayayayayayayayayayayayayayayayayayayayayayaya
yayayayayayayayayayayayayayayayayayayayayayayayayayayaya
yayayayayayayayayayayayayayayayayayayayayayayayayayayaya
yayayayayayayayayayayayayayayayayayayayayayayayayayayaya
yayayayayayayayayayayayayayayayayayayayayayayayayayayaya
yayayayayayayayayayayayayayayayayayayayayayayayayayayaya
yayayayayayayayayayayayayayayayayayayayayayayayayayayaya
yayayayayayayayayayayayayayayayayayayayayayayayayayayaya
yayayayayayayayayayayayayayayayayayayayayayayayayayayaya
yayayayayayayayayayayayayayayayayayayayayayayayayayayaya
yayayayayayayayayayayayayayayayayayayayayayayayayayayaya
yayayayayayayayayayayayayayayayayayayayayayayayayayayaya
yayayayayayayayayayayayayayayayayayayayayayayayayayayaya
yayayayayayayayayayayayayayayayayayayayayayayayayayaya—

FUCK.

Man, I'm so sorry, you guys. We were super, *super* close there, like seven seconds away. But I just started getting all these urgent notes from Nigel the Editor on AOL Instant Messenger.

This right here is an official . . .

Real-Time Update

Okay, so he's saying that this record makes absolutely no sense, given the immutable laws of time and physics.

I mean, I guess that's your opinion, man. But who's the Doctor here? Yeah, I am.

And now Nigel says at this point in the book all my readers might not even understand the significance of "yayaya," so I should discuss its secret origin and what it means to me as a person and an elite competitor. He also keeps using the word "indeed" for no good reason.

I mean, it's really not that complicated. It's just the terrifying guttural scream I make whenever I feel it in my stones, you know? Like deep in my massive steel cojones, right? Like say you take out some skinny punk in *Modern Warfare* and it's *"Yayaya!"* or you knock back a brew with some of your buds and it's *"Yayaya!"* or you finally squeeze out a massive dump and it's *"Yayaya!"* There's no, like, secret to it. It's just fucking "yayaya," you know? It's universal.

You got *"Yáyáyáyá"* in Spanish. Then there's *"Farfegnugyäyäyä"* in German, and "יאיאיא" in Hebrew, which, remember, is read right to left.

All right, now Nigel the Editor seems a little frustrated. He keeps yammering on about why I can't just write a fun chapter about what exactly I'm a doctor of. Would that really be so hard?

FINE.

We *won't* set the "yayaya" world record, okay? We *won't* have the honor of making *history* right here and now, even though over *7.3 million people* were only seven seconds—seven fucking seconds!!—away from taking their rightful place in the Guinness Hall of Warriors.

But I'm not gonna write about what I'm a doctor of until I'm fucking good and ready. And you might wanna do a better job of staying on my good side, okay, bro?

No, that's not a threat. Not in the legal sense, anyway.

I'm just saying—we live in a dangerous world. Shit happens. Crazy shit. Sometimes it can be helpful to be friends with a six-foot-eight hyper-athletic Adonis who has access to the latest cutting-edge Google technology in tactical vests, 4K HD scopes, and armored Lamborghini Diablos with custom GMV 1.3 1040 W-2 M5 Browning machine-gun turrets.

That's all I'm saying. That and—

Yayaya!

Okay, done.

(*Ya!*)

CHAPTER 3

THE TWO-TIME

I woke up this morning, put on my white silk robe—the only thing I own that's not slate black or blood red—and walked in front of my wall-sized mirror, letting my robe flutter open and fully exposing my butt-naked body.

I was on my way to my trophy room. It's the part of my multimillion-dollar Top Secret Command Center I visit about six or seven times a day, just to soak in the glory of all my success. It's really more of a gigantic hall than a room, because let's be honest—I need a lot of square footage to fit all 19,226 of my plaques, victor's cups, life-size golden statuettes, commemorative spears, and rare opals awarded to me by various dukes, sultans, and emperors.

But even with all these riches, even with all these honors and fine exotic spices and oils, nothing comes close to the prize that sits at the very top of the heap. There, underneath a domed skylight of the purest Tiffany crystal, with all these powerful red lasers shooting down and cool strobe lights and this mysterious mist that honestly, I don't even know where it comes from—there is my plastic trophy from the 1993 Blockbuster Video Game Championship. It kind of looks like a popcorn box with a VHS tape coming out of it, all coated with this metallic bronze finish, you get the idea.

And next to that trophy, except a tiny bit higher, is one from the 1994 Blockbuster Video Game Championship, which pretty much looks the same as '93's, except for the year.

And above those two is a special trophy that Blockbuster made right after I won the second championship, just because they were so impressed that I won them both back-to-back, and that one also pretty much looks the same as the other two.

And above those three is this special commemorative trophy they gave me in 1999, to mark the five-year anniversary of my incredible back-to-back domination. That one is another bucket, except this time they've got a Sony LaserDisc coming out of the popcorn box, you know, a real sign of the Blockbuster commitment to cutting-edge technology.

And then above those four is another commemorative trophy they gave me for the eight-year anniversary of the five-year anniversary, I'm not really sure why, and this one just has a little index card in the popcorn box that reads "Fuck Netflix," and they got the date of the inscription wrong by eleven days, but hey, you don't get to be a Fortune 50 company like Blockbuster without thinking outside the box, am I right?

Anyway, the point of all this, in case you're too chubby and out of shape to get it, is that I'm the Two-Time, Back-to-Back 1993–94 Blockbuster Video Game Champion, and it's the biggest deal in all competitive sports anywhere on the planet.

Now, I know what you're thinking.

You're thinking, "Doc, we get that this is such a prestigious prize, because the name Blockbuster stands for the quality and innovation and success of a timeless Fortune 25 company. We get that your level of dominance in winning such a cutthroat tournament not just once but *two times in a row* is absolutely unprecedented. We get all that. But tell us, Doc, why does your back-to-back Blockbuster Video Game Championship mean so much more to you *personally*? As a god-man among men?"

Well, if you'd stop interrupting me with all these damn questions, I honestly would've told you all of that like ten minutes ago.

The truth is this award isn't about only the glory or the prestige or even the destruction of my enemies. It's about the hero's journey. *My* journey. From no one to someone. From little guy to big guy. From small-town star to the biggest gamer the nation has ever seen.

It's about the suffering I endured, the trials I overcame on that hard and lonely path.

Like the young hawk when he first spreads his wings and soars through thunder and lightning to reach the tippity-top of the mountain. Like the baby anaconda when he wriggles out of his skin and slithers through fire and broken glass to strangle his first man-prey. Or like Fred Savage when he embarked on his epic cross-country road trip of victory and mayhem in that classic masterpiece of video game cinema *The Wizard*.

And if you don't get that reference, LOOK IT UP. Shit, kids these days!

It all started, as all great things did back in 1993, with a night out at Blockbuster Video. I was just eleven, but by now I was already a stunning physical specimen, a little preteen Zeus, standing at five foot five with three pounds of hair cascading down my back like bubbling black steel and a thick layer of ebony peach fuzz above my upper lip that I called Slick Junior.

By this time, Dr Disrespect was a local gaming legend. I dominated every pool hall, arcade, Sega Genesis, and Super Nintendo around. I even found the few tools who owned Sega CDs and I beat their asses too. Everyone could get it.

But I was getting too big for this town, baby! I was bored with my success, tired of being so damn superior to every gamer around, sick of being the biggest fish in such a teeny, tiny little guppy pond. And besides, people were starting to look at me kind of funny in my wraparound shades and my child-sized tactical vest. By which I mean five-foot-five children, because I was huge.

I needed to break out of that place and find a way to dominate on an elite national stage, but I didn't know *how*.

The only thing I had, the only thing that made any kind of *sense* anymore, was hanging with my bros at the local Blockbuster.

Now, let me tell you about Blockbuster Video back in '93, okay? You think Netflix is big? You got yourself a little hard-on for Hulu or Pluto or Fubo? That streaming crap has nothing on Blockbuster in the nineties, all right? Nothing!

Those big ballers with their blue-and-yellow logo and their Twizzlers and Milk Duds and their New Releases wall told us to make it a Blockbuster night, and we *made* it a Blockbuster night. Tuesday night, Wednesday night, Saturday night for all the virgins out there, which was all of us—they were all Blockbuster nights. We stood there and we looked at those rows and rows of *Home Alone 2*s and *Jurassic Park*s, and we stared at Sharon Stone on the boxes of *Basic Instinct* and got our baby boners, and we flashed those little laminated membership cards, and that was power, baby! That was freedom! That was the $1.99-video-rental experience, even if all that effort got you was a copy of *Hudson Hawk* that no one wanted! That, my friends, was Blockbuster.

There was just one problem on that steamy August night as I stood outside those glass doors with Ramrod and One-Eyed John and Steve and Razor Frank, who I think was actually Ukrainian in this dimension,* and I stared longingly at *A Bronx Tale*—and with more than a little interest in *The Piano*, because I had a weird thing for Holly Hunter.

I couldn't go in. Because I'd lost a video.

That video was *The Wizard*, starring teen prodigy Fred Savage.

If you still don't know, *The Wizard* is the most seminal coming-of-age-video-game-road-trip-movie-that-Fred-Savage-made-in-1989 of all time. Fred Savage and his little freaked-out brother make an *awesome* death-defying voyage across the country so the kid brother can compete in this colossal video game tournament in California and become the *greatest* gaming champion the world has ever known.

It's powerful, riveting entertainment. Siskel and Ebert gave it five thumbs-up, and I'm pretty sure Rex Reed called it "a manifesto of epiphanies." It inspired me, dared me to dream of something greater than my tiny little town, and if you still haven't watched it yet, do it right now, you lazy little punk.

Also, I didn't actually lose the video. I just wouldn't give it back, because the movie was that fucking good.

---

* Note: The contents of this story take place in Dimension V, coincidentally the same dimension where all the stuff in *V: The Final Battle* actually happened in real life. Some details may not apply to Dimensions 1, R, and #;K@1}`, or whatever dimension you're currently inhabiting at this exact second.

The late fee was so damn big by this point I couldn't even show my face in Blockbuster. I was straight-up banned, man. But I *could* see the gigantic cardboard sign they'd posted right by the counter—for the very first, one-time-only . . .

Blockbuster Video Game Championship.

And guess what? This tournament, with elite competitors coming in from all over America, was taking place at Marine World, in California.

California! Just like in *The Wizard*.

My eleven-year-old jaw, already so damn angular it could cut glass, just dropped. This was what I had been waiting for. I was gonna ditch this two-SNES town and go on my very own epic journey across the nation to prove myself at the biggest, most Block-busting video game tournament of all time. Just like Fred Savage in the *Apocalypse Now* of video-game-road-trip movies.

I mean, so what if I already lived in California? So what if my house was only a fifteen-minute walk from Marine World and the only thing my stupid little town was known for was that it offered really convenient parking for Marine World? You think I let that bullshit stop me?

It was meant to be. I was gonna hit the sidewalk and make my name.

I sat my parents down for a little talk. I was pacing in front of them in my tactical jacket and wraparound specs, and I was like, "Mama, Papa, Dr Disrespect isn't like the other little eleven-year-olds out there in He-Man pajamas still afraid of the boogeyman and the top bunk."

"But you *love* He-Man!" Mama protested.

"Dr Disrespect is his *own* man," I said, gazing into the middle distance. "And I'm gonna hitchhike by myself across the country, and at night I'm gonna sleep in burlap sacks on the side of the road, and during the day I'm gonna play video games for food and cold, hard cash, and I'm gonna compete in the Blockbuster Video Game Championship in Marine World, and I don't care what you say!"

Then my parents looked at each other kind of funny and they were like, "Um, honey, we'd be happy to just drive you to your tournament in our Dodge Caravan. It'll only take five minutes. Remember we were just there last weekend for the Bubbles the Killer Whale Show?"

And I was like, "OF COURSE I KNOW IT'S ONLY FIVE MINUTES AWAY! BUT I'M DR DISRESPECT AND I'M GONNA TRAVEL THE WORLD AND BE A NATIONAL MEGASTAR LIKE FRED SAVAGE IN *THE WIZARD* AND YOU CAN'T STOP ME!"

And they were like, "That Fred Savage seems so nice. We loved him in *Karate Kid*."

And I was like, "That is Ralph Macchio! But I get it, easy mistake."

And they were like, "Okay, you can do this, but we're following you in the car."

So I hit the road like the warrior I was, with nothing but my switchblade comb, my overdue copy of *The Wizard*, and a turkey sandwich my mom fixed. Oh, and also my He-Man pajamas, because they really are the baddest PJs ever made and I'll fight anyone who says different.

The journey was a hard one, my friends, I won't lie.

Except for my parents, there were no cars around to hitch a ride from. So I walked and walked and walked, my champion's heart pounding, the sweat pouring down my chiseled prepubescent body from the tippity-top of my head to the tips of my toes.

And that was after just four blocks. Shit!

"Are you sure you don't want to get in, uh, Doctor?" my mom called from the Dodge Caravan with its plush comfy seats and frosty-cool air-conditioning on full blast.

"Yeah, I'm sure! I will not ride to my destiny in America's safest minivan!"

"Okay, dear, but you really should've taken a left two blocks back."

"I did that ON PURPOSE!"

And I did do it on purpose—I swear! Because honestly it was like less than a fifteen-minute walk from my house to Marine World, and if I wanted a true odyssey of hurdles and challenges, I needed to go at least four miles, give or take three miles.

But after all that walking, all that epic journeying, I was starving. Hell, I was a growing boy at five foot five, with abs so hard you could use them to wash your Underoos. I checked my pack and remembered I'd already eaten my turkey sandwich three blocks ago, while still in my driveway.

"Are you hungry?" my mom shouted from the Dodge Caravan. "I packed a Lunchable for you!"

"No! This is part of the struggle!" Damn, that Lunchable looked delicious.

Then I looked and saw ahead, like it was fated to be, a seedy, grungy old saloon full of hard boys and biscuit-boxers. I could go inside and challenge some shark to a video game and win enough for dinner, easy peasy.

I pushed open the grimy saloon doors and strode up to the dirty old dude at the counter.

"Hey, I'm looking for some action," I said under my breath. "Competitive game of *Mario Kart, Double Dragon, Ninja Gaiden*, pick your poison. Fifteen bucks a match. I'll even give 'em a handicap."

He looked at me. "You realize this is a Denny's, right?"

I glared at him through my wraparound shades. "Fine. One game of *Donkey Kong* for a Moons Over My Hammy."

"Sheesh, kid," he said. "We don't even have video games here. But if you're hungry, I'll give you something to eat." He frowned. "Wait a second, aren't you Paul and Diane's kid from down the street?"

"THE NAME IS DR DISRESPECT AND I'M A HUNGRY WARRIOR TRAVELING THE COUNTRYSIDE ON MY WAY TO NATIONAL VIDEO GAME GLORY LIKE FRED SAVAGE IN *THE WIZARD!*"

And he was like, "That Fred Savage seems so nice. I loved him in *Teen Wolf.*"

And I was like, "That is Michael J. Fox. But I get it, easy mistake."

And he said, "You, uh, sure you don't want an apple or a cookie or something?"

"Chocolate chip?"

He nodded and handed me a cookie.

"Thanks," I said. "The Doctor won't forget your generosity when he's a national icon."

Just like that, I was back on the road. And the journey was a hard one, my friends, I won't lie.

Except for my parents, I was all alone in this cruel, uncaring world. I walked and walked, my muscle-bound legs growing weary, like a powerful but grumpy camel crossing the vast Sahara. I finally decided it was time to bunk down for the night.

I threw my pack down onto the cold, hard ground and started

to change into my He-Man pajamas. They were not only badass but also very warm and snuggly. I'd just stripped off my tactical jacket, my pants, and my Spider-Man Underoos when I heard the shouting of what I assumed was a crazy idiot.

"What the hell are you doing butt-nekkid on my front lawn!?" screamed the crazy old man. Even as angry as he was, I could tell he was impressed by my athleticism.

"How else do you expect me to bunk down for the cold, pitiless night?" I said.

"Night? It's twelve fucking noon! Now get your pasty ass—" He squinted. "Hey, aren't you Paul and Diane's kid from down the street?"

"Hi, Stan!" my mom called from the Dodge Caravan. "Sorry for the intrusion! Our son is a little . . . different."

"THE NAME IS DR DISRESPECT AND I AM ON A HISTORIC JOURNEY OF EPIC VIDEO GAME DOMINATION JUST LIKE FRED SAVAGE IN *THE WIZARD*!"

And Stan was like, "That Fred Savage seems so nice. I loved him in *Webster.*"

And I was like, "That was Emmanuel Lewis. But I get it, easy mistake."

I grabbed all my shit and I booked out of there—the Blockbuster Video Game Championship was going to start in just thirty minutes!

After all my wrong turns, all my epic adventuring, how the hell was I gonna make it? I didn't even know where I was!

Suddenly, like a Chariot of the Gods, racing down the road came the answer I'd been waiting for. The Lift of Destiny. The ride that would bring me to the end of my personal odyssey of fame and fortune.

A blood-red 1991 Lamborghini Diablo.

Now *that* was the way to travel.

I sprinted after it as it drove by—thankfully my highly developed calves and preternatural speed made me more than a match for its 5.7-liter V-12 engine. Also it was stuck at a red light.

"WAIT!" I screamed, waving my powerful arms. "HELP ME! I NEED A RIDE TO THE GREATEST BLOCKBUSTER VIDEO GAME CHAMPIONSHIP THE NATION HAS EVER KNOWN! HELP ME, PLEEEEEEASE!"

The sleek, tinted driver's-side window slowly went down.

And guess who was at the wheel?

Fred MF-ing Savage, that's who.

"Fuck you!" Fred Savage said. "I hate children! Now, stay away from my beautiful car and go to hell!" And just like that, he rolled up his window and peeled out in a cloud of smoke.

I couldn't believe it. Fred Savage was not that nice!

I dropped to my knees in despair, just as my parents pulled up next to me in the Dodge Caravan.

"Mama, Mama!" I wept. "Help me! Fred Savage seemed so nice in *The Wizard*! And *The Wonder Years* too! My life is a lie—I don't think I can make it to the end of my quest!"

"But you're standing at the entrance to Marine World," my mom said. "Like, five feet from the door."

I looked up and peered through my tears. "OF COURSE I KNEW THAT, MOM!"

My competitive fire was rekindled! My quest for greatness burned hotter and angrier than ever before! So I got up, dusted myself off, and walked proudly through the giant metal doors. Right after I borrowed $50 from my parents for the entry fee.

Inside was the most massive, epic arena of battle I had ever seen. Mightier than the Colosseum of Rome, more ancient than Stonehenge, more alien than Area 51, and truly worthy of two of the greatest Fortune 12 companies of all time—Blockbuster coming in at number six and Marine World trailing just behind it at number eight.

In front of me was a vast hall full of row upon row of state-of-the-art Sony Trinitron TVs. There must've been two or three hundred of those babies—all glowing and flashing like every one of their 640 x 480 pixels was alive. And man, back then, that was a shit-ton of pixels.

The place was teeming with thousands of competitors from all over the nation, like a Model UN minus every country except for America. There were slick snipers from New York City, oiled-up console surfers from Hawaii, and thirty-two-bit cowboys from the dusty plains of Wyoming, all there to prove their mettle on the big stage.

Press was swarming everywhere. Radio, newspapers, network TV, satellite TV, pay-per-view TV, *TV Guide*, everyone. We're talking Peter Jennings, we're talking Tom Brokaw, we're talking Wolf Blitzer—but no one really knew what CNN was yet, so even Connie Chung treated him like a bitch.

Music was blasting—BLASTING—from these huge Bose speakers hanging from the ceiling. Classics like Bel Biv DeVoe's "Poison," Lionel Richie's "Hello," and pretty much everything by Roxette (and I go la la la la la I've got the look).

And in the back looming behind it all, encased in an entire football field of thick protective glass, there was Bubbles the Killer Whale, arching and flexing in the icy blue water, baring fifty-six razor-sharp teeth, his glossy black eyes devoid of compassion. I never did find out how he saw out of those tiny eyes—it must've been his warrior spirit.

"Bubbles!" I shouted in my rage frenzy. "*Bubbles!* Give me your ruthless warrior spirit! Bless me with your killer instinct as I devastate my foes, earn honors and kippers beyond any gamer's wildest dreams, and avenge my roadside humiliation at the hands of Fred Savage, who it turns out isn't that nice!"

And lo, Bubbles spurted a victory geyser of spume into the sky and unleashed the unholy screech of a thwarted Nazgûl.

At that instant I turned and saw the Champion's Platform, all decked out in rich Blockbuster blue and gold. There at the podium, standing next to this old wrinkled rich white dude who must've been Mr. Blockbuster himself, was none other than my newest nemesis, that asshole Fred Savage.

Mr. Blockbuster gazed out at the throngs of competitors and wheezed into the mic.

"Hello, everyone, I'm Mr. Blockbuster. I'm standing here with Fred Savage, honorary master of ceremonies and star of *The Wizard*, to kick off the greatest gaming competition the country has ever seen, the one-time-only Blockbuster Video Game Championship!"

Everyone applauded and Bubbles the Killer Whale thrashed like a caged Leviathan.

"*And* to launch Blockbuster's new and improved Nintendo video game rental lineup!"

So yeah, turns out the whole thing was just this big promotional stunt to advertise Blockbuster's expanded Nintendo video game rental business. That's why they tied it all into Fred Savage and *The Wizard*, which was not only the greatest video-game-road-trip-coming-of-age movie of all time, but also one gigantic product-placement ad for Nintendo. The whole commercial aspect of the championship totally sullied what should've been a sacred torch of pure competitive fire, and I was furious. (Also make sure you go to InterdimensionalChampionsClub.gg for the latest in Official Dr Disrespect Apparel™ RIGHT FUCKING NOW!)

Anyway, then that asshole Fred Savage took the mic and smiled his phony Savage smile.

"Now, let the tournament—and the amazing deals on *all* Nintendo products at *your* local Blockbuster—begin!"

The competition was intense, my friends, I won't lie.

All right, that would be a lie, because I totally destroyed everyone. I mean, the other dudes were great and all, don't get me wrong, but I was the Doctor. The Almost-but-Not-Quite-Yet Two-Time. I was slicker than New York City, more cocoa buttery than the Hawaiian Islands, and I brought polygons to a Wyoming sprite fight.

But here's the thing. It wasn't just my unparalleled prowess with a joystick that gave me the edge. It wasn't just my skill at *The Legend of Zelda* and *Ninja Gaiden* and *Mike Tyson's Punch-Out!!* and every other Nintendo game ever created.

No, what truly made me superior to everyone else at that tournament was the journey I'd taken to get there. No one else had struggled the way I had. No one else had walked the roads for miles on end. No one else had scrounged for food at a hard-luck Denny's or battled psychos in the street in his He-Man pajamas.

Instead, they drove there in their fancy cars or flew there in their private jets or whatever it is that soft men do. Or, in the case of the Wyoming guy, I guess he really did backpack all the way from Wyoming to Marine World, but whatever—who won at *Mario Kart*? So fuck him.

I'd looked down that long, scary, dark alleyway of fear and I kept on pushing ahead. And that strength I gained, that experience, that *toughness* drove me past every competitor, through every round of the tournament—the quarterfinals, the semifinals, the semi-semifinals, the Sweet Sixteen, the Final Four, the Two of Hearts (Two Hearts That Beat as One). I won them all handily.

Up on the Champion's Platform, surrounded by thousands of screaming fans, with klieg lights shining down and Cypress Hill's "Hand on the Pump" slapping on the giant Bose speakers and Brokaw and Jennings and Wolf covering our every move and Bubbles the Killer Whale ramming against the glass of his big-ass aquarium, my very last battle was about to begin.

"All right, everybody!" Mr. Blockbuster announced to the crowd. "I'm very proud to present this glorious faux-bronze popcorn-box trophy to the *champion* of the one-time-only Blockbuster Video Game—"

"NO!" I screamed. "THERE'S ONE MORE ROUND! I WANT SAVAGE!"

These would be the real finals. My own private finals.

Mr. B and Fred Savage just kinda looked at each other. My parents, who were sitting in the fifth row, sighed audibly—like, I could actually hear them over the deafening music.

"But, uh . . . ," Mr. B said nervously. "You already *won*. You're the *champion*. There is no other round."

"NO!" I yelled. "ME AGAINST SAVAGE! RIGHT HERE, RIGHT NOW!"

"But-but I'm just the honorary master of ceremonies," Fred Savage stammered. "I'm horrible at video games!"

"NO! I SAW *THE WIZARD*! YOU CAN'T TRICK ME!"

"But I'm not even the character who was good at video games in *The Wizard*—he was played by my costar, Luke Edwards. And he's horrible at video games in real life too!"

"I DON'T CARE! I WANT TO BATTLE YOU NOWWWW-WWWW!"

They all covered their ears because they couldn't handle my volcanic anger. My parents looked absolutely humiliated. Even war correspondent Wolf Blitzer looked uncomfortable. So what? I was on a mission!

"Look, son," Mr. B said. "Can we please just give you your trophy so we can all go home and make it a Blockbuster night?"

"I don't know," I whispered. "*Can* you?"

And at that moment I reached into my bag and pulled out my ace in the hole. I held up my overdue copy of *The Wizard*.

"And the name isn't 'son,'" I said, "it's Doctor-octor-octor Disrespect-ect-ect-ect."

Mr. B gasped and whipped out the scanning gun he carried at all times. He read the bar code and his face went pale.

"I'm sorry, Fred," he said. "This is a problem. This overdue charge is higher than the value of Blockbuster LLC. This puts everything on the line!"

I laughed long and loud, the greatest diabolical-evil-villain laugh ever produced by an eleven-year-old boy. Then I stopped suddenly and looked at them both, dead serious.

"We settle this with trial by combat. Me against Savage. If I win, I get the video for keeps—and I get Fred Savage's Lamborghini. If I lose, I'll return the video that is now worth more than your whole company."

Fred Savage crinkled his nose like a precocious child actor. "What? How do you even know I have a Lambo? Who did you say you are?"

"Trust me," I said with a smirk. "After I'm done kicking your ass, you'll never forget."

So that asshole Fred Savage and I sat down on the Champion's Platform, with thousands of people watching, and cameras flashing, and C-SPAN airing us live on channel 57 (out of fifty-seven total), and we played *Super Mario 3* for reasons that'll be obvious to anyone who's seen *The Wizard*. And that should be everyone, because I have been very clear about this!

Anyway, I'd love to tell you the play-by-play of the epic, vicious, bloody battle between me and Fred Savage, but he was telling the truth—he really did suck at video games. Seriously, like, Mr. Block-buster could've beaten him. My mom could've beaten him. Hell, Bubbles could've beaten him using his flippers.

The funniest part of all was that Fred Savage was really, *really* trying to win, you know? Like, even though he knew he sucked, he was scrunching up his face and trying to concentrate while he played. And every time he screwed up—which was constantly—he'd make grunting sounds and say things like "Gosh darn it all!" and "Focus, Fred! Focus!"

I mean, I guess I could've given him credit for not giving up when facing a superior competitor like myself. But I knew that un-derneath all his bogus boy-next-door charm was the same asshole who'd left me in the dust during my time of need.

So instead I just laughed, absolutely *obliterated* him, and de-manded the keys to his Lambo when I was done.

"Did you actually think I would give you my car?" he said. "You're not even old enough to drive! And I never agreed to that bet!"

"Whatever," I said. "I shoulda known an asshole like you would back out."

"Why do you hate me so much?" he asked.

I turned and looked out at the thousands and thousands of people in the crowd. "You know," I said, "I guess I should actually thank you. I came a long way to get to this championship. Dealt with a lot of shit on the lonely road that you and Corey Woods, your character in *The Wizard*, couldn't even dream of. But nothing was harder than when you cursed me out and left me to die.

"But you know what?" I said, grabbing the collar of his polo shirt, which was buttoned to the very top. "It only made the Doctor *even stronger*."

"Wait, wait, wait," he said. "That was *you*?"

"Oh, so glad he *finally* remembers!" I shouted to the crowd. (I was being sarcastic.) "The man who screamed, 'Fuck you! I hate children! Now, stay away from my beautiful car and go to hell!' *finally* knows who I am!"

"I didn't say any of those things!" he said. "I shouted, 'Somebody help me! A naked maniac with incredible athleticism who's holding some pretty cool He-Man pajamas is accosting me!'"

"Well," I said, "that does sound a lot like me."

"You came out of nowhere!" he said. "This angry nude boy with superhumanly taut muscle tone just running and screaming like a madman. It was horrifying! I-I guess I didn't recognize you now with your wraparound sunglasses on."

"But *I heard you*!" I roared.

"I don't even *use* the F-word!" he said. "I say 'fudge' when I get upset, which isn't often."

"Huh," I said.

"In fact," he said, "as soon as I drove away I even used my car phone to call the police and the local psychiatric authorities to tell them a disturbed naked youth with highly developed calves needed counseling pronto."

I looked out at the crowd and saw a pair of cops and a couple old dudes in white lab jackets with clipboards standing around. They smiled and gave me a supportive thumbs-up.

"Well," I said. "You can see how I could make that mistake. What you said and what I heard sound very similar."

"No, not really."

"Wow," I said. "So you're really *not* an asshole! You really *are* a nice guy!"

"Yeah," he said, smiling. "I really am a nice guy."

I handed him my copy of *The Wizard*—which I now officially owned—and a pen. "Can a fan get your autograph?" I asked.

"Of course," Fred Savage said. "Anything for a fan."

I gave him a firm handshake. When it was all said and done he had been a worthy competitor.

The crowd cheered. My parents breathed sighs of relief. I fist-bumped Wolf Blitzer and wished him well with the whole twenty-four-hour-news thing, which sounded like a stupid idea.

Most important of all, I really had finally broken out of my small town, even though I'd only walked five minutes away from my house. I had my very first popcorn-box-with-a-VHS-tape-stuck-in-it trophy, and just like that I'd become the most famous, dominant gamer in America.

And guess what?

Blockbuster was so freaked out by the way I'd highjacked their one-time-only promotional tournament that they decided to hold a second one the following year. They wanted to give someone "normal" (lame) a chance to win.

So I came back and won the whole thing all over again. That pissed them off, so they announced they'd never hold one of their wildly successful national tournaments again. This was yet another example of why Blockbuster is the smartest, most timeless Fortune 3 company in the world. They're just waiting for Netflix to make one wrong move before they come roaring back to dominance.

Unfortunately, Fred Savage couldn't make it back for the 1994 championship, but I did get my parents to drive me there in our very own onyx-black Lamborghini Diablo. I may have even convinced them to let me take the wheel myself for a block or two. Yeah, it was a rental, but if there was one thing I knew, it was this:

I was the Two-Time, Back-to-Back 1993–94 Blockbuster Video Game Champion. Traveling any other way no longer made sense.

CHAPTER 4

GROOMING WITH THE DOCTOR

A lot of people have a problem with how incredibly seriously I take my grooming.

They say things like "Doc, true champions only focus on winning," or "Real men don't care about hair product," or "Bro, stop combing your mustache, you're about to drive your Lambo into that helpless pedestrian!"

And I say, "You don't know a damn thing about winning," and "I'm the manliest man you'll ever meet in your pathetic, unattractive life," and "That old lady with her little dog shoulda got the hell out of my way."

Because here's the thing.

It's not enough to only win, all right? You gotta win and you gotta *look good doing it.*

Think about it. Imagine you go to a tournament—and it can be any kind of tournament, okay? It can be video games, javelin throwing, Parcheesi, whatever—and you somehow manage to win. But when you do, you're not looking good.

So you get up there on that pedestal when it's all over to accept your medal, and guess what? No one wants to *celebrate* you. No one wants to take pictures of you. No one wants to talk about you or write about you or even look at you.

Why would they? You look like *hot garbage*! Your haircut is sensible and utilitarian. Your face is covered with razor bumps or gross pubey stubble. Your teeth are yellow and you smell like the wrong end of a dog. The truth is, you lost this thing before you played a single round.

Now imagine that I, Dr Disrespect, the Two-Time himself, am at this same tournament. And imagine—now, brace yourself here, because I'm about to say something ridiculous—imagine I actually come in second.

I know this makes no sense and you probably got a migraine just trying to think about it. My computer actually overheated when I typed it, like I literally just had to restart my Dell Inspiron prototype with Intel 980000 processing and WordPerfect 5.1 emulator, that's how completely, totally stupid it is to ever think of me coming in second in anything. Including javelin throwing or Parcheesi, because I'm excellent at both of those.

But anyway, for the sake of argument, let's pretend I did.

So at the medal ceremony I'm standing next to you, the "winner," on my slightly lower pedestal (not that it really matters, because I'm eleven inches taller than you, but whatever), about to get my slightly smaller second-place trophy.

Technically my award is inferior to yours, right? Technically my accomplishment is less than yours—you, the skinny, scraggly, pimply, sweaty winner.

But what happens when everyone sees me? What happens when the media takes in the sumptuous waves of my jet-black hair spilling over my broad, sculpted shoulders? What happens when all the fans get a look at my mustache, a.k.a. Slick Daddy, a.k.a. the Ethiopian Poisonous Caterpillar, with its aerodynamic lines and fearful symmetry?

What happens is that the camera bulbs flash and the video rolls, the line for selfies and autographs gets longer and longer, cars stop in the road and helicopters shelter in place, choruses of children sing hymns to my mullet, men from faraway lands give Slick Daddy exotic nicknames like Kaderin Dudak Kılı, which means "Lip-Hairs of Fate" in Turkish, or La Moustache Inconvenante, which I haven't gotten around to translating yet but I'm pretty sure is, like, Swahili or something.

Now, you tell me—who *really* won?

Also keep in mind that while we're standing next to each other, I use my superior athleticism to play keep-away with your first-place trophy and you can't do a thing about it except swing your arms uselessly while I palm your forehead like a basketball.

Who *really* won? That's right, you did. But no one cares!

And that's why these grooming tips are so fucking important.

PROPER MULLET CARE

Look, I'm the last person who's surprised that mullets are making a comeback right now. If anything, I'm surprised it took people thirty years to catch on.

Just this morning I spotted Tom Cruise, Leonardo DiCaprio,

and the guy from the Dos Equis Most Interesting Man in the World commercials. They were all grabbing a latte together at the Starbucks in front of my multimillion-dollar Top Secret Command Center, and they were all rocking mullets.

So I was like, "Hey, boys, nice hair."

And they were like, "Yeah, Doc, we're copying you."

And I was like, "Respect."

But know this—it takes a lot of time and effort to get your mullet ready for public viewing, all right? I've been tending to the liquid black steel tumbling down my back since I was a lion's cub in the art of hair styling. This shit ain't easy, or else everybody would be doing it. It's an art form.

Now, if I see you walking around out there with a shitty-looking mullet, it'll make me puke—so if you're gonna try this, I want you all in. Don't do it for you, do it for me.

1. Length

The ideal length of the back of any man's hair should *just* reach the third vertebra on his thoracic spine. That's the T3, for my fellow doctors out there. Not your T2, not your T4, and *definitely* not your T5. You're not the Feral Kid from *Mad Max 2.*

If you don't already know exactly where that is—and you should!—just use your fingers to count the nubs on the back of your neck. If you can't feel any nubs, that means you need to get your out-of-shape neck to the gym immediately.

Now, I can't emphasize this enough: it's very important to get this length exactly, *precisely* right. I've personally conducted doz-ens of in-depth scientific experiments to get the perfect length of the male mullet for critical mullet-utilizing actions, including:

a) whipping the ends of your hair in your enemy's face right after you make a witty comeback in an argument

b) proper flow and waviness when dancing to "Poison" by Bell Biv DeVoe

c) covering your eyes during a nap

d) hiding essential items behind your neck, like a switchblade comb, a zip gun, or the keys to your Lamborghini Diablo

e) world domination

2. Conditioner

The right conditioner is essential for maintaining an elite level of shine, sparkle, richness, and texture in your mullet. It might look to you like my hair is pure, jet-black beauty. But the truth is it's actually a *thousand* different shades of black. Some layers of my hair are onyx black, some are ebony black, some are charcoal black. Some are slate black, some are carbon black, some are coal black. Some are Vantablack, some are licorice black, some are blackness-of-space black. Some are black-hole black, and some are just really, really, really, really, really dark black.

There's also black-leather-jacket black, and black-pearl black, and black-mirror black. And blackstrap-molasses black, and squid-ink black, and storm-cloud black, and night-shadow black.

Like a million different facets of a thousand-carat black diamond, they are all layered and intertwined and cascading in a perfect symphony of liquid perfection.

And the *conductor* of that symphony? The conductor is my conditioner: Pert Plus.

It is actually a shampoo-conditioner combo, so it saves me five minutes in the shower every morning.

Pert Plus has this priceless, secret, all-natural ingredient you can only find in the most hidden depths of the rain forests of South America, called dihydrogenated tallowamidoethyl hydroxyethylmonium methosulfate. I'm pretty sure it was discovered by Magellan in, like, some rare Tibetan water lily. Then Pert Plus bought up the world's supply.

Every morning, smear that green, gooey goop into that scalp of yours, work it into a rich, hydrating, foamy lather, and watch while Pert Plus and its precious dihydrogenated tallowamidoethyl hydroxyethylmonium methosulfate clean and condition and highlight every single shade of luminous, glorious, sackcloth-sun black, volcanic-sand black, wetsuit black, or Vulcan-zombie black in your hair.

Unless you're a blond, which is a hair color for punks. I don't know why you'd even bother to wash that.

3. Combing

With hair as thick and bulletproof as mine, I don't actually have to comb it or blow-dry it. And I damn well don't have to perm it. It just kind of naturally falls into place with the perfect level of wavy undulation right after I shower.

So combing my hair isn't really about actual maintenance or adjustment—it's about looking really fucking cool. That's why only one tool will do: the switchblade comb. But here's the thing, all right? There are very specific, very precise ways to handle a switchblade comb, and if you get it wrong, honestly, what's the fucking point of life?

1) Okay, so first off, you wanna make sure you have a switchblade *comb* and not a switchblade *knife*. I don't have time to hear you bitch about your weak clotting.

2) Next, there's flipping it open. Before you press that button, make sure—**make absolutely 100 percent fucking certain**—that the comb is facing OUT and AWAY from your palm.

   You don't know how many attempts I've seen TOTALLY SCREWED UP when some idiot tried to flick the comb open and it just half popped out directly into their palm, and then they fumbled it and had to kind of toss it from one hand to another, and maybe they even dropped it on the floor, and immediately all the girls went home with headaches.

3) Third, there's timing. If you want to be running that thing across your hair with rhythm, you gotta *anticipate*, all right? You gotta know exactly when you need to pop that baby open on the two so you can have it cocked and ready to run through your hair on the four.

4) Last—and this is most important of all—there's placement of the comb itself.

   Because here's the thing. If you have cool hair, if it really is as thick and masculine and wavy as a tortoiseshell, you don't really want to actually *touch* your hair with the comb. You just want to give the *illusion* that you're *almost* combing your hair.

   You get that? Not even the illusion that you're combing. The illusion that you're *almost* combing. It's the air kiss of real men.

   So to do that, you want to keep a distance of 1.3 centimeters between the edge of the comb and your hair at all times. I repeat, AT ALL TIMES.

Okay. Now we're gonna put this all together and actually give it a try. We're gonna do an on-rhythm meta-illusional switch-blade-comb run through your long, thick, wavy, perfectly conditioned multilayered black hair.

Get that switchblade comb in your hand and . . . Deejay, drop it:

Bump-tsshhh.

Bump-tsshhh-tsshhh.

[Blade pop now!]

"They call him Doc!"

[Hair comb now!]

YES!

Excellent work! You did it on rhythm, with—

Whoa.

WHAT THE FUCK???

You forgot rule one of using a switchblade comb! **Make sure it's NOT a real switchblade!**

Fuck, now there's blood everywhere, and a chunk of your glorious new hair is just kind of lying there on the floor with like pieces of skin and some dandruff.

Though if I'm being fair, you still would've been good if you'd just followed rule four and kept the blade exactly 1.3 centimeters away from your hair. With that amount of blood, my guess is you shivved yourself at least half an inch deep.

But hey—take that little chunk of hair and guts with you. Maybe the surgeon can sew that shit back on. Shame to ruin such a good-looking mullet.

PROPER MUSTACHE CARE

All right, so the truth is that unlike mullets, mustaches still haven't exactly seen a revival.* And hey, who am I to judge? If you want a face like a baby, a woman, or a hairless cat, go ahead: free country. Not every dude is man enough to pull off a badass 'stache like Magnum, P.I., or Billy the Kid or Freddie Mercury or myself. If you're not on that level, I give you props for admitting it.

By now you know that's bullshit and I don't give you props for anything. But it's not too late to turn your life around, and by reading my book you've already taken an important first step.

Second step is to finally grow a decent goddamn mustache.

1. Style

You don't choose the right mustache for your face. It chooses you.

Now, I'm not saying that the spirit of Slick Daddy actually came to me in the night when I was a young, hairless, prepubescent superstar-in-waiting and whispered, "Doc . . . Doc . . . I'm here to show you the ideal mustache length and shape to complement your stunning square jaw and your proud warrior nose and your perfectly symmetrical face structure. Now, wake up and draw it on the official Dinobots stationery next to your bed so you know exactly how to sculpt me, Slick Daddy, when you get old enough for that kind of thing."

---

* The only mustache that counts in this dimension is the glorious, standalone, beardless mustache. Because once a mustache is attached to a beard, it's not really a mustache anymore, is it? It's just a guy who didn't shave for a while. Think about it.

But if I *did* choose to say something like that, that'd probably be pretty close to the spirit of what Slick Daddy would've told me, and I probably would've drawn a masterpiece of mustachioed art on my official Dinobots stationery.

And I'm actually using that original drawing—or, you know, would be if it really existed—to get Slick Daddy and his appearance trademarked, copyrighted, and patented all at the same time. So if you want to copy my mustache, you legally aren't allowed to, unless you pay me a licensing fee of $129.95 at Interdimensional-ChampionsClub.gg.

But, you know, there are plenty of other styles out there that are just okay, and I just know that at least one of them wants to choose your face.

So here's what you're gonna do.

You're gonna stand in front of a mirror, and you're gonna stare hard at that mug of yours, okay? Right at that naked spot above your upper lip. And you're gonna listen. Just *listen*.

Now, this might take a while, all right? You might be standing there two, three days. You might not be able to eat food or drink water, and you might have to wear an adult diaper.

But that's fine. That's ideal, in fact. Because sooner or later you're gonna hear a voice—just like I might have—and that voice is gonna whisper something to you.

Something like "handlebar" or "walrus" or "pencil" or "horseshoe."

That voice is your mustache choosing you. Or it's a fasting hallucination. But probably it's your mustache choosing you.

And you're gonna do whatever your mustache tells you to do, no matter how insane—with three important exceptions:

a) **The Hitler Mustache:** Most unpopular guy in recorded history, and honestly, if your mustache is whispering the name of any genocidal dictator, you should probably do an Amish beard instead.

b) **The Charlie Chaplin Mustache:** Great guy, but too weirdly close to the Hitler 'stache, so best to avoid.

c) **The Slick Daddy Mustache**™®© **(patent pending):** *Unless* you pay the $129.95 licensing fee at InterdimensionalChampionsClub.gg.

2. Razor

Look, the Two-Time doesn't use just *any* razor.

The brilliant mustache scientists at Schick developed for me and me only a special Mach 23 Prototype Razor XL-3000 with twenty-three—yeah, *twenty-three*—blades on it for the closest possible shave in the history of humanity on Earth or in space.

Now, I know what you're thinking, because you're not as clever as you assume. You're thinking, "Doc, Schick doesn't even make the Mach line of razors, that's Gillette."

But that's checkers to my chess.

See, I was about to give Gillette the honor of crafting a one-of-a-kind custom razor for Slick Daddy, but they couldn't figure out how to put more than nineteen blades on a single razor, and that's fucking unacceptable.

So I went to my boys at Schick and, yeah, even they were kind of confused by why I needed so many blades on a single razor, but I pointed at Slick Daddy and was like, "Fellas, you think a mustache this cunning, this deadly, doesn't know *exactly* what he wants? Are you really trying to tell me the Ethiopian Poisonous Caterpillar deserves *fewer* than twenty-three blades? *Are you?*"

They totally saw the flawless logic in my argument, and they also saw me cracking the knuckles of my huge, powerful, rocklike fists, so they were like, "You got it, Doc!"

Now the only razor that touches this sensitive yet stunningly square jaw is my Mach 23 Prototype Razor XL-3000 and its twenty-three blades of pure titanium, coated with diamond carbonite for maximum precision and sharpness to get within one-millionth of one-thousandth of one-hundredth of one nanometer of my skin.

Or in other words, the precise width of a single atom at the very bottom of my ball sack. Which actually is a pretty big fucking atom.

And just in case I get bored while I'm shaving—and because I'm really good at multitasking—each prototype razor is fitted with prototype Bose Micro speakers so I can listen to Bell Biv DeVoe's "Poison," *plus* a prototype mini 4K VR Sony plasma-screen so I can watch reruns of *Knight Rider*, *plus* an experimental prototype mini Nokia flip phone so I can take a call to close a monster deal, all while keeping my face baby-butt smooth.

Because these priceless prototype razors are engineered with exceptional custom bespoke Schick technology, each one is totally good enough for a single shave. After I'm done I throw it away and open up a new one.

A little pricey, yeah, but when you're the greatest gaming super-star of all time, a luxury like that isn't just a luxury—it's a necessity that's also really luxurious.

Oh, and for a normal guy like you? You can just buy a bag of a thousand Bics for like two bucks or whatever. Honestly, that shit's all the same anyway, right?

3. Nickname

Let's be real here for a sec, all right? Can you handle the realness?

The realness is this: Giving your mustache a cool nickname is just as important as making it look good. Maybe even more so.

Think about it. Looking great doesn't mean much if people aren't *talking* about your looking great. And who's gonna talk about your mustache if it has a shitty nickname or none at all?

Now, if you got a mustache named Slick Daddy—which, again, you never will because it's trademarked, copyrighted, and patent pending—then *everyone's* gonna want a piece of that thing.

Just *say* the words "Slick" and "Daddy" and you immediately think of a world-champion mustache that's perfectly groomed, thick, dominant, black, and attached to a man of towering height, sweet wraparound shades, and the latest technology in flip phones.

Seriously, just say it a few times out loud. No, honestly, like right now.

You feel that vibration? It makes you want to dance with the wolf and fly with the eagle.

It makes you ask, "What makes this guy tick? Would he ever be interested in what makes me tick?"

But here's some more realness for you, all right? Coming up with a nickname for yourself ain't easy. It takes the heart of a warrior, the cojones of a rhino, and the soul of Don Draper.

Matter of fact, Slick Daddy really did come to me in my dreams in the middle of the night to whisper his nickname in my ear. He had a voice like gravel soaked in scotch, and he spoke in a commanding way that pierced the inner reaches of my being.

Besides Slick Daddy, the only other person who ever nicknamed himself successfully was the late, great, ever-eternal Black Mamba, Kobe Bryant. And we both know you're not on his level, come on now.

But don't worry, you're in luck.

Not only am I a super-nice, perfect, modest champion, but I also happen to be really, really good at coming up with cool nicknames. So just this once—*just this once!*—my genius creative mind is gonna do all the work for you.

Below are two columns, Column E and Column N, because those are the letters I felt like. Pick one word from Column E and one word from Column N. Doesn't matter which two you choose.

Put 'em together and BOOM, you got a brand-new, custom-built, badass nickname for your mustache, just like that. Hundred percent guaranteed.

Shit, I'm good.

COLUMN E	COLUMN N
DEADLY	COBRA
KILLER	SNAKE
KILLINGEST	PYTHON
DEATHLY	VIPER
MURDERING	SPATULA
DEATH-MAKING	MICROWAVE
SPICY	SAUSAGE
LEFTOVER	PIZZA
EMPTY	BRITA
COLD	BEERS
BROKEN	TOASTER

Okay! Inspired work, if I do say so myself.

Just remember that it's always Column E *first*, then Column N. Never the other way around, because that would be ridiculous. Except maybe Cobra Killer, which is kind of sick.

Foreign Nickname Bonus Content

If you want some foreign nicknames for your mustache—and Slick Daddy seriously must have about twenty spanning all seven continents, all seven seas, and both polar ice caps (off the top of my head there's the Ethiopian Poisonous Caterpillar [obvs], the Spanish Picante Chile Con Carne, the Irish Swarthy Leprechaun, and the Russian Это Как Гугл Переводчик Работает Привет*)—well, then, you pretty much have to be a major international super-celebrity like me.

Sorry, that's just how it is.

Then once you're one of us, you get into your private plane or your personal Kamov Ka-27 attack chopper and you fly to every country you're famous in—all of them, if you're me—and you walk into a local sports bar in the last minute of a very important sports game and you stand in front of the only TV in the whole place and you scream at the top of your lungs, "NAME MY MUSTACHE! NAME IT NOWWWWWWWWW!"

Then after that, some local foreign guy who's totally drunk and out of shape stands up and shouts something in a language you don't understand. You record it on your flip phone, you politely say

---

* If you can't speak fluent Russian (like I can) in this dimension, LOOK IT UP. SHIT, **KIDS TODAY!**

thank you, and then you get the fuck out of there before he stabs you with a broken bottle.

And then you've got an official, authentic foreign nickname for your mustache.

PROPER BODY ODOR

This one is pretty simple.

You ever get that not-so-fresh feeling in the morning? Like you take your shower, you wash and condition your long, thick jet-black hair with Pert Plus, you step out and dry off with your loom-woven silk towel, and you think, "Man, I just don't feel so fresh this morning."

Fear not, my friend. Because for just those kinds of mornings— for every morning, really—I've got just the body spray for you.

It's **SLICK, BY DOC**.

I know, you can just hear that icy-smooth jingle I composed myself echoing in the background, can't you?

Bump-tsshhh.

Bump-tsshhh-tsshhh.

"Slick, by Doc!"

Of course you can.

SLICK, BY DOC represents the ultimate in masculine smells designed specifically for men. And not just any men—I'm talking men who know how to *win*. That's right, **SLICK, BY DOC** was formulated by the world's top odor scientists to be a precise blend of one-third testosterone, one-third musk, one-third violence, and one-third victory.

Just slap six or seven ounces of **SLICK, BY DOC** all over your butt-naked body twice a day, maybe even four times if you really like smelling great like I do, and you'll feel ready to dominate the universe on a whole new level of thunder and lightning and twilight of the gods.

Sound good? You bet it does.

Why wait any longer? Go NOW to InterdimensionalChampionsClub.gg and for the reasonable price of $1,399.99 you can order your very own lifetime supply of—

FUCK.

Sorry, you guys. I was really on a roll there, but my AOL Instant Messenger just beeped, and I got Nigel the Editor giving me an official . . .

Real-Time Update

Shit. This is the worst.

This dude is actually messaging me that the publisher is sick of all my "self-promotion" and "advertising." That they didn't give me this huge book deal so I could "peddle" my "cheap paraphernalia" on my "website," and I should stick to writing my "book."

First off, enough with all the written air quotes, all right, man? We get it.

Second, I don't even know what the fuck "paraphernalia" is, but whatever it is, mine *definitely* ain't cheap.

Is it my fault that **SLICK, BY DOC** happens to be scientifically proven to have more power, more energy, more WOW than any other men's body spray on the planet?

Is it my fault that my mustache, Slick Daddy, is so badass that I trademarked and copyrighted it, and everyone has to pay me $129.95 at InterdimensionalChampionsClub.gg if they want to copy it?

Of course not! I'm just trying to give the people what they want here! I'm doing the citizens of this earth a favor! They want access to the coolest, hottest body wash and the most advanced prototype merchandise in the universe, and I want to give it to them!

Did Dostoyevsky's publisher stop him from pushing the babushka? Did Shakespeare's editor stop him from telling the world about codpieces and merkins? Of course not! If the greats could do it, why can't I?

I—and **SLICK, BY DOC**, available NOW with **SLICK** *for Her*, **ALSO BY DOC** for the low combined price of $1,799.98 for a limited time only—am the greatest of them all!

All right, so now Nigel the Editor is messaging me that no one believes my nonsense, and if I don't stop hawking my stuff and start doing my job—in particular, writing about what exactly I'm a doctor of *immediately*—then the publisher is gonna reconsider this *whole thing.*

Whoa. I mean . . . WHOA.

Those are some bold, bold words, my man.

When you totally screwed up my longest-"yayaya" record, I let it go. It was hard, but I let it go. And that was a chance to make *history*!

But this time? I don't know, dude. You try to *threaten* me? Me—the Two-Time, the most dominant gaming champion the universe has ever known? You try to intimidate me? To bully me? You threaten to take away *my own book*?

A book I've poured myself into, fought for, bled for? A book I've been working on *nonstop* for at least an hour and a half after I got bored of doing much cooler stuff?

You think you can take that away from me?

Well, I got news for you, bro—I'm gonna take it away from *you*.

That's right, Nigel the Editor. This is it. This is the end of the book.

No secret founding of the Champions Club. No incredible tips on how you too can have an amazing vertical leap. And damn well nothing about what I'm actually a doctor of.

It's finished. It's over. I'm done putting up with all your, like, editing and shit.

This, RIGHT NOW, is the official conclusion of my highly anticipated first and only memoir, *Violence. Speed. Momentum.*

Oh wait. I guess I need the . . .

Acknowledgments

Thank you to MYSELF for being such a great sport about all this. I totally couldn't have done it without me. Later.

Yayayaya!

CHAPTER 5

ALL RIGHT, I'M BACK

Nigel the Editor begged for forgiveness and bought ten cases of SLICK, BY DOC, and I very graciously marked up the price by 120 percent and agreed to keep writing my book.

Way I look at it, this is a win-win-win situation, because I get tons of money, the boys at the publishing office smell great—or at least as great as bookworms can possibly smell—and you guys get to keep devouring all my priceless pearls of wisdom to give meaning to your otherwise pointless lives.

But I still haven't forgiven Nigel the Editor. I mean, I'll think about it. But some wrongs can't be made right, you know? Some fences can't be mended. I might seem invincible on the outside, but deep down . . . well, I'm pretty much invincible—but still, no one threatens me. No one tells me what to do, and no one, I mean no one, out-negotiates Dr Disrespect.

CHAPTER 6

THE DOC'S FIRST SPONSOR

Every big-time gamer remembers his first sponsor. Even gamers less big-time than me, and that's all of them.

To get that first paycheck with your name on it, *not* because you're flipping grease at a Burger-Rama or sitting in some shitty little cubicle with your clip-on tie, but because you're a stone-cold killer on an 8K battlefield of mayhem.

Because you're contributing something *real* and *powerful* and *important* to society—*video game dominance.*

That, my friend, is an awesome feeling. That is flying with the eagles through the storms and above the clouds and into the sun. That is the flavor of true success.

Of course, you look at punk-kid gamers these days, and they all got it easy. They're nine years old, they're eating their Mr. T cereal, they're munching on Pop-Tarts and chewing on Bubble Tape, and then they decide—"What the hell, I'm gonna jump on some new streaming platform and play a little Fortnite and see if I can get a few followers, why not?"

And the next thing you know, they're making six figures from some sports-energy drink based out of Shanghai.

But back when I got started in the nineties? Back before streaming wars and PS4s and 8K LCDs and 1080p's and Chinese sports-energy drinks with five billion yuan to toss at little punks?

Shiiiit, you had to *fight* to survive. You had to *earn* your keep with blood and violence and cunning. You had to *know* what you were worth and how to get what you wanted. And if you didn't?

Then you died.

Or maybe, I don't know, you got a real job, which is almost worse.

But *maybe* you literally died!

I know, because it almost happened to me when I got my very first sponsor.

———————

It was 1998. For the past few years, ever since I'd won my second Blockbuster Video Game Championship, I'd been taking accelerated, advanced prototype classes in high school during the week and traveling to tournaments on the weekend.

Thinking back, it must've been hard on the other kids in my class, having to walk the tiled halls in the shadow of a national celebrity like me. By the time I hit my teens I was already six foot four with the baby-oiled body of a Greek god, a fully grown Slick Daddy, a glorious, silky black-on-black-on-black mullet, and, of course, full body armor.

Then you had everyone else. A bunch of pimply turds in khakis and blue jeans. Their midsections flabby, their upper lips soft and sweaty, their faces covered in stress rashes from their next AP Calculus exam. I almost felt sorry for them.

Just kidding, I fucking loved it! And I aced AP Calc because I'm a Mensa-certified genius.

When that weekend rolled around? Man, I competed *everywhere*. I went to every tournament I could find, no matter where, no matter when, no matter how big or how small. I dominated the Radio Shack Videoganza in Orlando. I kicked ass at the Menahga, Minnesota, County Fair and Pinball Social. And I took no prisoners at the South Bronx Cyberdome, which for the bonus round had an actual back-alley knife fight.

My reputation grew. My fame grew. *I* grew—six foot five, six foot six, six foot seven, six foot eight. I was one big-ass dude.

But my bank account? That didn't do shit.

By the time I graduated, all I had left from my winnings was a cool scar above my kidney from the knife fight in the Bronx, the prizewinning 452-pound pumpkin from the Menahga County Fair, and all the time in the world to watch Fred Savage in *The Wizard* over and over again because I owned my copy.

Now there I was, sitting in a shitty little studio apartment I couldn't even afford, playing *Shaq Fu* all alone, doing the most uncool, un-Doc thing I'd ever done in my life. By which I don't mean playing *Shaq Fu* all alone—I mean feeling sorry for myself.

I'd always dreamed of having my own multimillion-dollar Top Secret Command Center, but instead I had a hot plate for a kitchen and an old shower curtain as a bathroom wall. I'd always dreamed of owning the most advanced Sony prototype audiovisual technology, and maybe even getting HBO, but instead I owned a fourteen-inch black-and-white Sanyo with tinfoil on the antennas. I'd always dreamed of owning forty-seven Motorola flip phones, but instead I only owned three, and they were Ericssons.

Also, I was hungry. That sucked the most. Hell, I was a growing boy-god and I didn't have a thing in my mini fridge! What was I gonna do—eat my prizewinning pumpkin? Of course not, pumpkin is disgusting, everyone knows that. And I couldn't eat my vintage autographed copy of *The Wizard*, could I?

I thought about my parents. Maybe I shouldn't have screamed "I'm gonna be the richest, most successful champion in the history of the world and I'm never gonna ask you for money! NEVER!" right before walking out the door forever.

I thought about my old friend Razor Frank. Maybe I shouldn't have shouted "I hate your stupid nickname and I'm never gonna ask you for money! NEVER!" right after he'd bought me breakfast that morning. Then again, I was pretty sure he only spoke Portuguese in this dimension, so maybe he didn't understand me anyway.*

I thought long and hard, and I had just started to open Ericsson flip phone number three to call my parents for help, when suddenly I heard a knock at the door.

Knock knock knock!

Who was that? No one interrupts the Doc when he is busy feeling sorry for himself, which is practically never. No one!

Knock knock knock!

All right, exception to every rule.

I stood up from my sofa, which was also my bed, dining table, and Top Secret Research Laboratory. I looked through the peephole and saw these two skinny little nerd-punks standing there looking totally harmless, kinda nervous, and mostly just really nice.

---

* Seriously, no fucking idea what dimension this is anymore. Let's call it Dimension Δ, just because mood: Greek demigod.

So I drew my eleven-inch hunting blade out of its sheath because I thought it would be fun to mess with them.

As I threw open the door I waved my razor-sharp knife and screamed, "WHAT THE FUCK DO YOU WANT!"

They squealed like little pigs and the one with the bushy eyebrows actually peed his khaki pants! And I laughed my ass off.

"I'm just kidding, guys," I said. "But seriously, what the fuck do you want? I am, like, super busy making diabolical plans to dominate the universe with my fleet of armored Lamborghini Diablos."

"I'm Larry," eyebrows guy said, "and this is Sergey. You must be Dr Disrespect."

Now I got suspicious again. The location of my Top Secret Command Center was top secret. How did they find me? There was only one rational explanation: they were government spies, sent to steal the secrets of my superhuman speed and reflexes.

"How the hell," I said in a low growl, "did you find my Top Secret Command Center?"

"Well," Sergey said, "first off there's this sign that's Scotch-taped to your door that says 'Dr Disrespect's Top Secret Command Center.' It looks like a dot-matrix printout with, I don't know, a clip-art graphic of Nyan Cat or something—"

"That's a vicious puma!" I snarled. "And I've been *telling* the library they need a laser printer!"

"And second, you're listed in the phone book. First name 'Dr,' middle name 'Dis,' last name 'Respect.'"

I looked Sergey dead in the eye for five. Long. Minutes.

"So," I finally whispered, "you're *not* here to steal the secrets of my superhuman speed and reflexes?"

"Um, no?" Sergey answered.

"Awesome, love it," I said. "You guys wanna come in? That's my sofa/bed/kitchen table/Top Secret Lab. Take a load off. Larry—can I call you Lare?—here's a towel for your pee-pee pants. No shame, brother."

Of course I was lying and Lare totally should've been ashamed. I tossed him a rag, and they sat down.

"Doc," Sergey said, "Larry and I own a small start-up named . . . Oogle."

"Great name," I said.

Then I started hacking and gagging like I had a hairball, because that name sucked.

"Um, thanks," he said. "Our start-up makes video game hardware, and we're a few months away from launching our very first product—a high-end multisensory, variable-input joystick that'll revolutionize gaming forever."

"Better than a Sony prototype?" I asked.

They paused dramatically. "Yes," Larry said. "Even better than that."

Wow. This was legit.

"We've been planning the rollout," Sergey said, "and you've come to our attention over the last few years, starting with your incredibly impressive Blockbuster Video Game Championship—"

"Plural! Back-to-back," I said. "'Ninety-Three *and* 'Ninety-Four."

"—and, frankly, your rather interesting, uh, personal style choices."

"You mean the black steel, silky and bulletproof? I guess you could say it revolutionized the hair game. Wanna run your fingers through it?"

"No, thank you," Sergey said.

I laughed loud. "I was messing with you! I'd never let a punk like you touch my hair. You're lucky I even let you hear that joke."

Sergey said, "Larry and I thought that a, uh, character such as yourself would make a fun, cool ambassador for our brand-new product."

I eyed him with the sonar vision of an eagle.

"So," I said. "You *are* here to steal the secrets of my superhuman speed and reflexes. *I knew it!*"

Sergey and Larry kind of looked at each other.

"No," Sergey said. "Why do you keep saying that?"

"Isn't that what being your 'ambassador' means? That you sponge off me like a parasite?"

"No," he said. "When we say 'ambassador,' we are thinking, like, maybe you could use our controller at your next tournament. Or maybe, I don't know, we put a photo of your mustache on the box for a small fee or something."

"Yeah!" Larry said. "That would be fun!"

I couldn't believe my ears. "My mustache, Slick Daddy, *sell out for a fee*?" My stomach grumbled loudly and I continued, "You're goddamn right he would! That mustache has no morals. None! The Ethiopian Poisonous Caterpillar is a total cash whore."

Sergey cleared his throat. "Yes, well, keep in mind that we're a very small company."

"Very small," Larry said.

"Ten million dollars," I said. "In unmarked one-dollar bills."

"Absolutely not," Sergey said.

"Okay," I said slowly. "Ten million . . . pennies! Also unmarked!"

"No," he said.

"What if they were *marked* pennies?"

"Still no."

"Lunch!" I shouted. "A ham fucking sandwich! Right now! There's a goddamn diner down the block! I haven't eaten since breakfast! I'm starving to death here!"

"Sorry," Sergey said.

"*But*," Larry said, "we are prepared to offer you . . . a ten percent discount on our revolutionary new multisensory, variable-input joystick. The same one you'll be advertising!"

"Uh," I said.

"Fine!" he said. "Twelve percent!"

"Wow," Sergey said. "You're busting our balls here, Doc. Brutal negotiation."

"Oh," Larry added. "And that discount only applies to a single purchase. And it's nontransferable."

"So," Sergey said. "We've got a deal?"

I stared at them with a gaze of raging fire. Cracked my iron knuckles. Clenched my perfectly square jaw. Felt the blood thundering through my veins. I was Dr Disrespect. I was worth so much more than this. But still—I was broke and hungry, and the last thing I wanted to do was admit defeat to my parents. Plus Sergey and Larry really did seem like nice guys . . .

Finally, I nodded.

"Yeah, we got a deal," I growled. "But watch your tone with the Two-Time."

"Excellent!" Sergey said. "Now, if you could just sign this contract—totally standard, just gives us all rights to use your image, likeness, name, and physiological essence throughout the universe in perpetuity—we'll be all set. Here, I've got a pen."

Sergey handed me the contract. Nothing major, just a couple

hundred pages in Latin. Then the pen, which he handled very carefully. They watched eagerly as I signed my name. I started to put down the pen . . . when suddenly everything began going dark.

"Take the knife out of his hand," I heard Larry say right before I blacked out completely. "We don't want a damaged specimen . . ."

When I came to, I was strapped down tight to an exam table in some kind of secret lab. Blinding lights shined down on me, and electronic devices beeped and buzzed from the shadows. Electrodes were attached to my forehead, and all these wires and tubes ran in and out of my hands. It was like when Drago is hooked up to all that evil Soviet science crap in *Rocky IV*, except I'm a ton more shredded than Dolph Lundgren.

I strained against my bonds as hard as I could, but they wouldn't give. Surprising, because I'm a ton stronger than Dolph Lundgren too.

"I've studied you well, Dr Disrespect," a voice said from behind me. "All your moves, all your maneuvers and tricks—the video of your many tournaments is quite extensive—and those bonds have been engineered to resist even your superior strength."

He stepped in front of me. Pale and skinny, with watery gray eyes and a long white lab coat, he looked even geekier than Larry and Sergey. But overall still like a pretty nice guy, except for the kidnapping and medical experiments.

"Where are Sergey and Larry?" I demanded. "What the hell is going on here?"

"Sergey and Larry are out meeting with venture capitalists," he said. "They get to do all the fancy glamour-boy stuff. It's scientists like me who get stuck doing the real work, building the actual products."

"You mean . . ."

"Yes," he said. "We've been working for years to build the prototype for the ideal video game controller, but we finally realized that something was missing. One critical final ingredient. The ideal video game *player.*"

"So," I said, "you really *are* stealing the secrets of my superhuman speed and reflexes?"

"Obviously."

"Motherfucker!" I shouted. "I knew it! Larry and Sergey kept giving me all this shit about it. Like, '*Why do you keep saying blah-blah-blah?*' And I'm like, '*I don't know, seems pretty spot-on to me,*' and they're like, '*Blah-blah-lie-lie-lie.*' Fucking pricks!"

"Yeah, villains lie," he said. "Between you and me, I've been searching for another gig for the last couple months. Not as easy as you'd think to find work as a sadistic scientist these days. I'm Paul, by the way."

"Nice to meet you," I said. "I'd shake hands, but you know—tubes, straps."

"Yes, of course," Paul said as he pressed some buttons on one of his machines.

"That pen they handed me did something to knock me out, didn't it?"

"Indeed," he said. "I invented a microscopic delivery system that injected a powerful tranquilizer through the pores in your fingers."

"Man," I said. "That's awesome."

"Thanks," he said. "It's nice to feel appreciated."

"Look, Paul," I said. "You seem like a nice enough dude. I mean, you could probably stand to do some squats, but whatever, I get it—you're a science guy. Not everyone is as naturally athletic as I am.

"But here's the deal. If you don't let me out of here in five seconds, I'm gonna have to break out. And if I have to break out, I'm gonna have to hurt you. Now, I don't *wanna* hurt you, but I mean, you are experimenting on me against my will, and I am a blood-thirsty battle hawk. So, from one doctor to another—let me go, or shit will get real."

Paul laughed. I think he was going for a diabolical, evil villain laugh, but honestly it was pretty lame.

"You're an exceptional human being, Doc," he said. "I not only admit that—it's the very reason you're here. But I have an exceptional mind, and there's no way you're breaking out.

"Now, if you'll just hold still a bit, these tests I'm about to run will help us shape and mold our controller to the precise, Platonically ideal standards of your unusually large hands, while calibrating the response ratio of our AI input-output fields to the precise biometrics of your nervous system. It should only take three or four weeks."

I shrugged. "Your funeral, bro."

Never taking his eyes off me, Paul the Scientist picked up some kind of control panel and started turning dials and pushing buttons. The machines around me began to buzz and beep even louder, and I could feel waves of electricity coursing through my body.

My muscles spasmed, my eyelids started fluttering faster and faster, and every hair on my body stood on end. Slick Daddy took on a life of his own, doing this crazy-ass caterpillar dance right under my nose. Pretty cool, actually.

I was pissed. I knew I shouldn't be here—I was *better* than this. Yeah, I was broke. Yeah, my only TV was a black-and-white Sanyo. And yeah, I had been starving since breakfast.

But to make a deal with two nobodies off the street for nothing but a nontransferable 12 percent discount off a goddamn joystick? That wasn't me. That wasn't why I'd left home. I'd left the nest to become a warrior. To be the most dominant gamer in the history of the universe. And I knew it.

"My God!" Paul said excitedly, glancing at the readout. "I've never seen biometrics like this before! We can do so much with this information—so much! Screw joysticks. We can cure cancer . . . create the perfect sports-energy drink and launch it in Shanghai . . . clone an entire army of identical supersoldiers . . ."

That finally did it.

I mean, curing cancer would be cool. And who wouldn't want the perfect sports-energy drink? But create more than one Doc? An entire *army* of Two-Times? What would that even be? Four Thousand and Thirty-Eight–Times?

Doesn't matter, man. There can only be *one* Dr Disrespect.

Focusing all my energy, all my rage, I flexed every wildcat muscle in my six-foot-eight frame. The noise from the machines became deafening, lights started flashing, alarms blaring everywhere.

"Amazing!" Paul shouted. "You're off the charts! I literally have to create a new chart right now!"

He turned toward a monitor and I saw my chance. I pulled against my bonds with everything I had, every ounce of strength, every molecule of my being.

CRACK!

The straps exploded, and like lightning streaking through the night sky, I jumped off the exam table, drew a hidden blade out of my secret ankle sheath—why do morons *never* check for a secret ankle sheath?—and whipped it at Paul's head.

THWACK!

The blade point pierced the collar of his lab coat, missing his face by millimeters and pinning him to a wall of instruments with a burst of sparks and smoke.

Paul the Scientist gulped so loud I could hear it five feet away.

"Doc," he said, trembling, "can I have your autograph?"

"You got it, Paul." I laughed and punched him in the face, breaking his nose with a sickening snap, his blood spurting everywhere.

I used his blood to sign my name on the wall and then I walked out.

The lab exit door opened, and I couldn't believe my eyes.

This top secret lab was right in the middle of Stanford's campus! I should've known—goddamn entitled college kids. Nice campus, though. Lots of trees.

And walking right out from behind a couple of those trees were my old friends Larry and Sergey.

"Hey, fellas," I said as I pulled out my second ankle blade— seriously, why does no one ever check for those?

They froze.

"Oh shit," Sergey said. "I knew we shouldn't have let Paul handle such a big project."

The light of the afternoon sun flashed across my blade. "Sorry, boys," I said. "But I'm done fucking around." I took a step toward them, blood in my eyes and violence in my heart. Surprising literally no one, Larry pissed himself again.

"You really gotta see someone about that, Lare," I said.

"Please, Doc," Sergey said. "Please don't hurt us. We just wanted to bless the gaming world with a superior controller, that's all!"

"We had no intention of being evil!" Larry said. "We swear!"

I sighed and lowered my weapon. They were lucky that I wasn't in a killing mood. This time.

"Here's what really pisses me off, guys," I said. "You didn't even have to drug me with a poisonous pen and lock me up in your lab to steal the secrets of my superhuman speed and reflexes. You could've just asked! I mean, it's kind of flattering, when you think about it. I woulda said yes just for the fun of it, you know?"

"Well," Sergey said, "we were thinking of just asking. But then you kept being like, '*Oh, you're here to steal my blah blah blah, right?*' So we were like, '*Huh, stealing—sounds like a good idea blah blah.*'"

"And let's be honest," Larry said. "Taking people's data in a sneaky underhanded way is a lot more fun than just, like, asking for it openly and transparently—even if they would give it to you willingly in order to improve service."

"And," Sergey said, "you *did* sign away the rights to your physiological essence. Even if it was buried in the middle of a long and complicated contract."

"That's fair," I said. "You got me on that one."

"But look," Sergey said. "No hard feelings, all right? As our apology, we'll give you a full *twenty percent* off the controller we'll base on your own personal biometrics. And a .015 percent ownership stake in Oogle."

I threw back my head and laughed long and hard. "Are you kidding me?" I said. "You may have tricked the Doc once—a total ridiculous miracle, by the way—but you won't get him twice. Your stupid start-up won't amount to jack. Especially with a dumb-ass name like Oogle."

"Well," Larry said, "we have been thinking of changing it to Google."

"Come on!" I shouted. "That's even worse!"

"Great talk, Doc," Larry said. "So if that's everything, we'll just be on our way . . ."

Slowly they started edging away. In a flash, the serrated blade of my knife was inches from Larry's throat.

"*I have one more condition,*" I whispered menacingly. "*And it's nonnegotiable.*"

They stood there, trembling.

"I want that ham sandwich we talked about earlier today."

"That . . . that was actually a week ago," Larry whimpered. "You've been out for a while."

"Whatever," I said. "I am *so* goddamn hungry, it's crazy. Must have something to do with destroying your lab and breaking Paul's nose with my bare hands while maintaining a superhuman metabolism."

His hands quivering, Larry pulled out his wallet and gave me a twenty-dollar bill. For exactly 1.2 milliseconds I thought about giving him a firm handshake—but I decided he wasn't worthy and would possibly straight-up poop his pants if I touched him.

So instead, I got myself a delicious ham sandwich for lunch.

Of course, like I predicted, their stupid video game controller was a total flop. Never even manufactured a working prototype. It was simply impossible for them to mimic my skill, my timing, or my reflexes with their advanced artificial-intelligence processors. Technology just can't handle the unique excellence that is Dr Disrespect.

A few years later Larry and Sergey did end up doing something else, something pathetic like search engine optimization, nothing cool like video games. Apparently my .015 share of the company would've netted me something like, I don't know, $72 million or something?

But you know what? It was totally worth it. Never again would I forget just how much I was worth. Never again would I let someone push me around in a negotiation. Never again would I lose sight of my one true goal of absolute world domination.

And best of all, that ham sandwich really hit the fucking spot. If I close my eyes and concentrate, I can still taste it.

CHAPTER 7

THE SECOND TIME I DROVE A LAMBORGHINI (AND HOW YOU CAN DRIVE ONE TOO)

Why does it always have to be "the first time I did this, the first time I did that"?

If I want to write in gripping, powerful detail about the *second* time I drove a Lambo, that's what I'm gonna do, and you're gonna like it. Got that, Nigel the Editor?

So it turns out that the second time I drove a Lamborghini Diablo happened thanks to my second professional sponsor. Yeah, the circle of life is a beautiful thing, people. Soon after I taught the nerd-punks at Oogle a lesson they probably forgot immediately, I was approached by Popeyes with another deal.

They offered me a lifetime all-you-can-eat supply of Popeyes fried chicken, and all I had to do was go on TV, bite into a drumstick, and say, "My name might be Dr Disrespect, but there's one thing this Doctor *does* respect, and that's Popeyes fried chicken. It makes the minimap in my mouth go *craaaaazy!*"

But since I'd learned my lesson, and the Two-Time doesn't forget, I refused to do a thing for them unless they paid me a cool half million dollars and changed my line to "My name is Dr Disrespect, and I'll eat this crapola because they're paying me."

Guess what? The morons went for it. All the suits kept babbling about how much they loved my "authenticity" and could I please remove my serrated hunting blade from their jugular, and they signed then and there. Again, that's on them for not checking my secret ankle sheath.

So not only am I still able to eat as much Popeyes as I want to this day—and honestly, those sandwiches are like fried heaven—but I also got to replace my black-and-white Sanyo with a color Sanyo, to buy new curtains for my little shithole apartment, and to blow *all* the rest of my money on my very own brand-new completely blacked-out 1998 Lamborghini Diablo.

And if I'm being honest, the Lambo was so damn expensive I actually had to borrow an extra twenty bones from Razor Frank just to close the deal.

Now, look, I know what you're thinking: "Doc, is it really wise financial planning to spend all your money on a high-performance gas-guzzling exotic sports car when you can barely afford to eat?"

And for once I'm actually happy for the interruption because:

1) If you were paying attention, you'd know I'd just earned a lifetime supply of delicious Popeyes chicken, so all I ate was fried chicken morning, noon, and night for every meal of the day until my veins were pumping pure gravy, and feathers were

coming out my pores and my nose until I could barely breathe and I thought I was gonna die. So that was awesome.

2) You clearly—CLEARLY—have never driven a Lambo.

I know this because the moment I drove a Lamborghini Diablo for the very first time—remember that? Back when I rented one to get to my second Blockbuster Video Game Championship back in 1994?—I knew that I would not stop, would not rest, would not even truly *live* until I owned my very own Lambo. I'd do anything to get my hands on one, all right? ANYTHING! And no one who's actually driven a Lamborghini for themselves could possibly feel any different.

Driving a Lamborghini is like injecting pure violence, pure speed, pure momentum directly into your aorta. Everything you do, the very reality you experience, is transported to a whole new level on the cosmic plane.

Step into the driver's seat and you're in a Chariot of the Gods. Turn the key in the ignition and watch the phoenix be reborn in a burst of flames. The engine rumbles and you feel the vibrations in your loins, the earthquake in your soul. Grip the steering wheel and you're wrestling with a bloodthirsty panther. Then you put your foot on that pedal and—

BOOM! The thunder!

BOOM! The lightning!

BOOM! The energy!

Then you drive to the 7-Eleven for Zima and beef jerky and instead arrive at the tippity-top of Mount Olympus for manna and ambrosia.

Now, don't come to me being like, "Oh, but, Doc, I've driven a Porsche before!" Or a Ferrari! Or a Jaguar or an Aston Martin or any kind of super-duper speedy-speedster you think might be kinda the same thing as a Lamborghini.

NO! IT'S NOT.

You can take your Porsche, all right, and you can put it on top of your Ferrari, and you can put that inside your Jaguar and wrap all that in your Aston Martin like some kind of crazy sports-car turducken—and it *still* wouldn't be half the automobile the Lamborghini is. They're just not on the same level of spiritual ecstasy.

But here's what I'm gonna do, because I like you—or at least, I pity you.

I'm gonna help you experience the might, the majesty, the magnificence of driving a Lambo all by yourself for once in your sorry, flabby, pear-shaped life.

You're not even gonna have to buy one. You're just gonna have to pretend to.

All you gotta do is follow *every last one* of these diabolical, devious, extremely well-researched steps:

1. Find an Authorized Lamborghini Dealer

This dealer should be close enough to you so your shitty 1973 AMC Gremlin can make it there without, like, exploding, but not so close that anyone who works there will know you or have legal jurisdiction over crimes you may or may not commit—so, you know, cross the Hazzard County line!

2. Buy a Reliable Stopwatch

I recommend an advanced prototype Timex T7G51002 for extra reliability. It should cost you about $3.99 at Walmart.

3. Formulate an Illegal Poisonous Compound Using Common Household Ingredients ████████████████████ [redacted]

Fuck. What is this? All I wanted to do was type ████████████ ██████████████ [redacted]—SHIT!

All right, guys, I had a feeling this might happen.

Because I'm both a killer assassin *and* a doctor—I won't tell you of what, not yet—I know how to make a certain illegal poisonous compound that induces *rapid excessive nosebleeds*.

It's critical to my plan, and it's actually pretty simple to make.

But Nigel the Editor and the suits at the publishing house won't let me—ME—write down the key ingredient, ████████████████ ███████████ [redacted]. Some garbage about liability and we'll all go to jail for five hundred years blah blah blabbity blah blah.

So listen.

Go to the dark web, and look up common household ingredients that cause rapid excessive nosebleeds, all right? You'll see ███████████████████████████ [redacted] listed right there. You all have it. Trust me.

Once you have the ███████████████████████ [redacted]— shit, so annoying—just take ██████████████ [redacted]—come on, seriously?—and use a mortar and pestle to grind them up into a very fine ██████████ [redacted]—bro, are you kidding?—then mix that with ████ [redacted] milliliters of █████████████████████ [redacted]— DUDE, IT'S ████████████████████ [redacted]!! YOU CAN GET IT FROM YOUR LOCAL FUCKING ██████████████ [redacted]!— and then put ████████████████ [redacted] in ████ [redacted] small ██████████████ [redacted] ████████████████ [redacted].

MOTHERF█████!!!

Whatever. Dark web, nosebleeds. You get it.

4. Makeover Time

Lamborghini dealers are obviously classy, posh dudes who are used to dealing with high-net-worth clientele. So if you wanna *drive* a Lambo, you gotta *look* like a guy who drives a Lambo.

Bonus tip: the more you *look* like a guy who drives a Lambo, the more you'll *feel* like a guy who drives a Lambo. In other words, a winner.

a) *Take a shower.* If I know you, and I think I do, you need one bad.

b) *Do all the grooming tips from chapter 4.* I mean all of them: Pert Plus, **SLICK, BY DOC** body spray, mullet, 'stache, the whole deal. Those last two might take a while to grow in. That's cool, I'll wait.

c) *Get dressed.* You wanna dress in a way that shows you're not only rich enough to buy sweet clothes, you're so damn rich you don't have to. I find that a skintight black T-shirt with a solid-gold-plated medallion around my neck generally impresses people. And if it happens to be a warm day, go ahead and put on those cut-off black jean shorts. Nothing cooler than showing off a pair of well-oiled, nicely tanned calves.

d) *Get swole.* Look, who are we kidding? You're a chubby slob. That's not gonna change overnight. But we can at least tone a little, right? I want twenty squats now. NOW! Come on, target those glutes, baby! Target those glutes! Now give me twenty push-ups, fifty crunches, thirty pull-ups—WITH PERFECT FORM—and thirty RDLs, and run five miles for the hell of it. What, you're complaining? Shit, I do this ten times as my warm-up. Not even my warm-up for working out. My warm-up for having lunch. BUCK UP!*

    e) *Repeat steps a through c.* Because now you're all sweaty and you stink. We can't have you go to the Lambo dealer like that.

5. Drive to the Lamborghini Dealer

Park your '73 AMC Gremlin at least four blocks away so no one can tell it's your car. Bonus points if you park right under a bird's nest so your car gets covered in shit, because that's hilarious.

    If the posh, snooty dealer asks you where your ride is, be like, "My chauffeur dropped me off in my slate-black stretch Hummer with flame detailing on the sides." That'll shut him up.

6. Browse the Merchandise

The key here is to act like an incredibly successful, hyper-dominant winner at all times. I know, it's a stretch.

    Start by super-casually looking at the floor models. Like you're barely glancing at them out of the corner of your eye, you're in the middle of a super-important call on your Motorola flip phone, and you hardly even know why the fuck you're there.

    Every now and then, just happen to notice the sticker price on one of the models' windows. When you see it, arch an eyebrow really, really subtly, then laugh extra loud and shout, "THAT'S IT!? THAT'S CHEAP AF!"

---

* Whatever dimension you're in, talk to your doctor to see if your lazy ass can actually handle real exercise. Because in my dimension, I'm not liable for *any of that shit* if you have a heart attack.

Make sure you say "AF" and not "as fuck," because that's much classier.

Then, right as the posh, arrogant sales dude walks over—you'll have to fight him off because you look like such a boss in that solid-gold-plated medallion—I want you to say super loud into your flip phone, "Tell Mendoza that if he doesn't raise the bid by five mil, the deal is *off*!"

When the sales dude gets to you, hold up a finger in his face like you need a minute. Make sure it's not your middle finger. Into the phone be like, "Uh-huh. That's what I thought."

Then snap the phone shut, look the posh sales dude dead in the eye, and go, "Sorry, you know how Swiss bankers can be." Laugh and slap him on the back way too hard.

When he asks what car you're looking for, say, "I don't know. What day is it?" Then when he tells you, say, "I knew that." Then when he looks at you funny, say, "The most expensive one you got." When he looks at you funny again, be like, "The 2021 Lamborghini Aventador SVJ, black-on-black-on-onyx-coal-death-black, just like I said five minutes ago, you skinny punk."

And if that doesn't make the right impression, you may be a lost cause.

7. Slip Him the Mickey

I know, I know. "Slip him the mickey" sounds a little more late-night Cinemax than what it means.

But it's just an old-timey phrase people used back in the 1600s when they wanted to put a poisonous illegal substance in a Lambo salesman's drink to induce a massive nosebleed.

Anyway, now that your posh slick salesman knows that you're

a legit, high-net-worth customer who's totally a winner, he's gonna ask you if you want something to drink. They'll have an espresso machine because Lamborghinis are Italian, and Italians love espresso almost as much as envelopes of cash.

So you're gonna be like, "Yeah, make it a double espresso."

Now, you and I both know that espressos actually taste like shit. We're real American men who drink Folgers with Splenda and non-dairy creamer. But that's not what's important now. *Now* we need you to order that espresso, and we *absolutely* need you to make sure he's drinking one too.

So say something cool, like "I never drink my double espresso alone. So you better drink one too." Bonus points if you end with "*Capiche?*"

While your guy is getting your drinks, position yourself next to a vase full of orchids. Lambo dealers love vases full of orchids because they look expensive. As soon as he gets back, knock over the vase, scream, "YOU STUPID PUNK!" and while he's desperately cleaning up the mess, take his drink and pour in all of the illegal poisonous compound. Espresso is so disgusting, he won't notice any difference.

Then when he's done cleaning, hand him his drink and say, "To fast cars, world domination, and mysterious nosebleeds!" and watch him gulp it down.

8. Start Your Advanced Prototype Timex T7G51002 Timer

Assuming your posh, snooty Lambo salesman is of average weight and height, it'll take a little over *nineteen minutes* for the drug to take effect.

Program your timer for nineteen minutes, then hit start.

9. Kill Time

Nineteen minutes is about seventeen minutes longer than small talk will last, so here are some insightful, totally inconspicuous questions you can ask your posh sales dude to distract him while the illegal poisonous compound works its magic.

a) Just how many shades of black does Lamborghini offer anyway?
b) How's that nose of yours feeling?
c) Are you a weak clotter?
d) Do you currently take aspirin, Advil, Motrin, Nuprin, or Aleve?
e) Has it been nineteen minutes since you drank that espresso?

10. Secure Your Test Drive

When that timer finally beeps, shout, "FINE! I'LL TAKE A TEST DRIVE."

Then look over at the posh salesman's manager and shrug, like "Where did you find this guy?"

The salesman won't want his manager to think he's about to blow a deal with such a successful, high-net-worth dude, so he'll agree to give you the test drive immediately.

Once he does, you'll have just enough time to give him your license and get through all the BS paperwork before the sales dude's nostrils start to erupt like a blood volcano.

Driver's License Distraction
Bonus Content

At this stage there's one other issue that's almost impossible to avoid: your driver's license, and the fact that it very clearly states your address.

For me, that's 1 Rich Guy Street, Command Center Island, The Universe.*

Not a problem at a Lambo dealership.

For you, it's 86 Dumbass Lane, Shithole, USA.

Definitely a problem at a Lambo dealership.

Also, you probably still own the same Velcro Incredible Hulk wallet you've had since middle school. I mean, *I* think it's cool—but they might not.

So here's what you're gonna do.

Before you leave for the dealership, I want you to get out your Monopoly board game. That's the one that's shoved in the bottom of your closet with all the corners taped up, buried beneath Candy Land, Connect 4, Life, and Operation with the funny bone missing.

Take all those pink, orange, and blue Monopoly tens, fifties, and hundreds and stuff them in that Velcro Incredible Hulk wallet.

---

* This is not my real address in any dimension. I'm way too smart to give out such confidential information to my thousands of enemies, and I'm way too cool to live on Rich Guy Street. I'd obviously only live on the much fancier Rich Guy Boulevard. Which isn't, uh, my real address either. So definitely do NOT Google Map that also-fake address if you're one of my thousands of enemies.

I mean, just cram 'em in there. Pack it so it looks like the Hulk is about to bust out with all that cash, all right?

Then, when the snobby salesman asks for your driver's license, pull out that wallet, rip open that Velcro, and *just barely* flash some of those funky bills. Wait till he kinda frowns, then laugh and casually say, "I really gotta start separating my yen from my rubles, you know?"

He'll be so impressed by what a legit international player you are, he won't even notice that colossally shitty address of yours. You're welcome.

11. The Moment of Truth

By now, you and the posh slick sales dude should be walking toward your diamond-black-on-steel-black 2021 Lamborghini Aventador SVJ.

You are on the verge of having an experience of divine religious bliss without equal in your life.

Your heart is pounding like an ancient Druid warrior on a ceremonial drum. Your armpit sweat is gushing like the mighty tributaries of the Amazon. The neurons in your brain are firing like a nine-volt Duracell.

You're about to reach a whole new level of smoke and thunder and speed and MORE SMOKE!

Your posh slick sales guy, on the other hand, is about to enter a whole new world of bleeding out.

His nasal passages are starting to feel a little crackly. There's a slight tickle behind his eyeballs, right in a spot he can't quite scratch unless he wants to pierce his retina. He's feeling a warm, sticky mess of goopy red fluid build in his sinuses and start to work its way down his nose.

That goopy red fluid, in case you haven't figured it out yet, is blood.

And the posh sales dude is looking at you, and he's taking you in. He's taking in your black ribbed T-shirt and your pure-gold-plated medallion. He's taking in your normally flabby yet recently toned physique. He's taking in your mullet and your mustache and your obvious mental imbalance and the fact that you had a bunch of what looked like Monopoly money stuffed in your middle-school wallet.

And he's thinking, "Can I really trust this absolute tool bag with my precious, irreplaceable, literally million-dollar vehicle?"

And before he can say no fucking way, the dam breaks and an eruption of blood bursts from his sinuses. He's trying to stop the flow by stuffing a fancy silk handkerchief up his nostrils, followed by deli napkins, gum wrappers, important legal documents, and crumpled paper from the garbage can, because now this is a fucking *gusher*. He looks at the precious, perfect Lambo and realizes the horror of even one drop of his blood touching that fine black Corinthian-leather interior. He screams, "DEAR GOD NO!" and just before he runs away sobbing and crying, in one world-shifting, timeline-twisting moment of truth—he drops the keys in slow motion. Right into your waiting hand.

And just like that, that Lambo is all yours. For at least five minutes, after which he will call every cop in the state to bust your ass.

So drive it, my man. Get behind that wheel, put the key in that ignition, and drive that baby like you've never driven before. Trust me—even while the cops are dragging you away, even while they're slapping the cuffs on your weak wrists and tossing your flabby, sorry butt behind bars for grand theft auto, you'll know it was all worth it.

And you'll never, ever again want to drive anything other than a Lamborghini.

CHAPTER 8

THE SECRET BEHIND WHAT, EXACTLY, I'M A DOCTOR OF

Yeah, that's right—it's finally here.

The question Nigel the Editor has been bugging me about ever since we first met at the New York City App Lebeés.

The question everyone all over the world always wants the answer to—I mean seriously, people stop me on the street, in the middle of E3, and even at the top secret Ralphs I do all my grocery shopping at, and they really do ask me this question.

They all want to know—Doc, what, exactly, are you a doctor of?

And look, I'll admit I've been a little cagey about it in the past, all right? I'll admit that I kinda enjoyed giving you all the run-around.

I'll tell people, "I don't know, maybe I'm a doctor of philosophy, learned in the ways of Plato and Aristotle and *The Secret*, with a top degree from DeVry University. Maybe I'm a doctor of psychology, because I'm always in my opponent's head. Maybe I'm a doctor of jurisprudence, because I lay down the law and then I break it. Or maybe 'Doctor' is just my first name on my birth certificate, designated legally by myself on the day I was born."

Depending on the person who asks, depending on the mood I'm in, depending on the dimension, I'll spew out a new answer like a fart in the wind.

Why not? I'm an arrogant dick, and it's fun to mess with you—so what else is new?

But guess what? I'm *not* an arrogant dick. I was just kidding. I'm a nice guy, a generous guy.

And that's why after all these years, I'm finally gonna give you and Nigel the Editor exactly what you want.

That's right, Nigel the Editor, I'm gonna forget about all your annoying interruptions and your corrections and your idiotic redactions of my illegal poisonous substances. I'm EVEN gonna ignore the absolute CRIME you committed, that TRAVESTY OF JUSTICE AND HUMANITY, when you threatened me—ME!—by saying you'd take away my book if I didn't stop hawking my merch. I'll even forget that you wear tweed.

Because I'm such a nice, caring, forgiving dude, I'm gonna let all that slide and give you exactly what you want—the secret knowledge of what, exactly, I'm a doctor of.

So here goes.

Here, at long last, is what I, the Two-Time himself, the man, the myth, and the legend, the Back-to-Back 1993–94 Blockbuster Video Game Champion, the greatest gaming superstar of the entire universe—here, finally, FINALLY, is what, exactly, I'm a doctor of . . .

Oh man . . .

Shit . . .

I just felt a rumble in the ol' tum-tum. A little jelly in the belly, if you know what I mean. A bubbling below deck. A rollin' in my colon.

What I'm trying to say is, to use a technical anatomical term, I feel a case of explosive, raging, vengeful diarrhea coming on right now.

And it's coming on in a way that is only a huge unfortunate coincidence and has NOTHING to do with the fact that I was just about to give Nigel the Editor *exactly* what he's been so desperately, so pathetically begging me for since the beginning of our acquaintance.

It must've been the leftover chicken wonton tacos from App Lebeés I just ate. Or maybe it was the brewpub pretzels with beer cheese dip. Or the double helping of Neighborhood Beef Nachos™.

Or maybe it's because all that food is over two months old. I don't know, I'm not an expert.

But whatever it was—fuck. All right all right all right all right. Emergency-time-emergency-time! We got an emergent emergency emerging right now!!

So sorry, Nigel the Editor—I'll be right back, just one sec, just gotta—

. . .

Whew! All right!

So yeah. As of right now, I am happy to officially report that all personal business is taken care of. I'm back in my top secret lab in front of my computer, and I am absolutely NOT currently sitting on the can typing this right now.

Of course not! How unprofessional that would be. How potentially destructive to the advanced Dell Inspiron laptop that's totally

NOT resting on my bare-naked Vaselined legs, just one false move from my entire un-backed-up book being lost, just like that!

No sir.

And now, just for Nigel the Editor, I'm back to that big, unanswered question, of what, exactly, I'm a—

Actually, hold up. While I'm definitely NOT typing this book while I sit on my black marble prototype Kohler KT-593261 with Experimental Turbo Flush™, there's something I've been wanting to get off my chest. Seems like now is as good a time as any.

As every true Doc fan knows, I'm already on the record when it comes to the whole wiping-sitting-down versus wiping-standing-up debate.

I understand that this debate has torn families apart and divided our nation. I know that it's more controversial than politics, religion, and the console wars. I get it.

But the Two-Time has never been one to shy away from controversy. I don't flee from the shadows into the light, and I don't hide from danger. I head right into that long, dark alleyway of fear and I keep on fighting.

So I have no problem saying to the world that I'm a wiping-sitting-down guy, and that anyone who actually thinks wiping their butt *after* they're already standing up—

Sorry. It's just such a ridiculous concept I had to laugh, and that chuckle most definitely did NOT make me squirt out another butt pee right now.

Anyway, if you wipe standing up, you're nothing but a round-shouldered, soft-jawed, pudgy-gut loser, and that's all there is to it.

My position on this is known, all right? I'm on the record.

But there's something more I want to address. Something new.

Something that's come to light in a certain dimension—I won't name names—because of a certain event called COVID-19.*

What happened is, we all got a little freaked out about the world's running out of TP, okay?

I know that some of you—**all of you**—stockpiled five thousand rolls of Charmin and Cottonelle and Scott and Quilted Northern and even that weird no-brand shit that fell off a truck and cost $15 at the hardware store. And even after you got those five thousand rolls, you went onto Amazon and Walmart and Target and you tried to buy even **more**, except there was no more, so what did you do?

You freaked the fuck out! Then you went ahead and you bought a bidet, didn't you?

Now every time you take your poop, instead of remaining seated and wiping your ass with TP like a red-blooded American, you let some creepy French or Japanese apparatus hose a jet of water **directly into your bunghole**.

I mean, have we completely lost it as a country? Have we forgotten honor, dignity, masculinity, and sacrifice? The beachheads at Normandy? The Boston Tea Party? The Declaration of Independence? Freaknik?

How can you possibly allow a foreign device to shoot water into your ass? Should we just start speaking German right now?

No, my friends, I'll tell you how we can stay true to our school. And that's by purchasing my brand-new, trademarked, patent-pending *American* bidet, **SQUIRT, BY DOC**.

That's right. **SQUIRT, BY DOC** is the only bidet designed spe-

---

* Yeah, with your luck it's probably your dimension. Sucks to be you.

cially by the Nobel-winning scientists at my multimillion-dollar Top Secret Command Center to spray water into your sphincter in the most dignified, dominant, and American way possible.

I know, because I most definitely did NOT just use it to deep-cleanse my muscular, athletic butt after an insane bout of powerful, explosive diarrhea while I'm typing this at this moment.

To own your very own **SQUIRT, BY DOC**, go NOW to Inter-dimensionalChampionsClub.gg—

FUCK.

Hey, sorry, guys. I just got a ping from Nigel the Editor on AOL Instant Messenger, and I have a feeling he's gonna be *pissed*. Oh man—I'm having a hard time not laughing and not butt-peeing again.

Anyway, I guess we got an official . . .

Real-Time Update

Yeah, so I checked my AIM, and here's what Nigel the Editor wrote:

Doc: I am indeed sick of all this fighting and your total lack of respect for me and everything I do for you and literature in general. I'm quitting your book and going on a two-week vacation to Hong Kong. Forthwith, Simon & Schuster will connect you with a new punching bag—I mean editor. Yours never, Nigel the Editor

Well. It was just, like, a joke, dude.

I don't really even *make* a bidet. (If I did, it would come in slate black and Lamborghini red and would be on sale NOW for only $99.95!)

Seriously, man, I was just messing with you. I don't even mind that you totally threw in "indeed" and "forthwith" in a fricking AIM message. Honestly, all your pompous crap was starting to grow on me.

But hey, it's your call. If you can't take my world-champion heat, then get out of my all-black-granite kitchen. And go on vacay to Hong Kong, I guess.

Hong Kong . . . Hong Kong . . . You know, that reminds me of another one of my never-before-told stories. And it totally coincidentally happens to be my next chapter . . .

By the way, that definitely was NOT the sound of a flush you just heard.

CHAPTER 9

THE KUMITE EXCEPT FOR VIDEO GAMES AND ALSO IT'S REAL

Part One: The Brotherhood

I've shared a ton of powerful stories in this book.

You, of course, have loved them all. You've laughed. Your heart has raced. You've cried at least a dozen times, and most of those times you didn't even know why. "Am I happy? Am I angry? Maybe I'm just really confused?"

Who knows? And who really cares? Not me, that's for damn sure.

But what I do know is that this story, the one I'm about to tell you, is the best one so far. Except maybe for that one where I did whatever it was in Dimension Whatever. Yeah, that was a great story, and this one probably isn't as good as that one, but it's still really fucking good.

It's the story of Doc—that's me—fighting the greatest enemy I've ever faced in my entire life: my own boredom. Also an ancient global criminal network of bloodthirsty killers run by the evil Lord Hannn, and their just-as-ancient illegal cutthroat international video game tournament called the Kumite Except for Video Games and Also It's Real (KEFVGAAIR), filled with the top gaming champions the world had to offer, not to mention thousands of other psychos and hoodlums with knives and guns and bazookas. But really my own boredom.

All right, so it was 2001. I was sitting there in my top secret lair one night toward the end of the year, staring emptily at my massive state-of-the-art 164-inch Fujitsu plasma TV.

Fuck, that thing was big. At least eleven inches bigger than my last Fujitsu.

I had just finished playing *Halo* for the very first time. It had just been released—not to the public, but to superstars like me—and it was revolutionary. First-person shooter. Multiplayer. 3D. Fast, responsive, intuitive, violent. Possibly the greatest game ever created. And using my advanced prototype experimental Xbox, I'd just hosted an online showdown between myself and the fifteen best gamers in America.

And I'd dominated them all. Because of course I did.

Because I'm the Doc. Because I'm the Two-Time.

Because duh.

I couldn't believe it. I was playing the greatest video game of all time against the greatest players in the nation, and I was fucking bored.

My campaign for Popeyes a couple years earlier, officially titled "My Name Is Dr Disrespect, and I'll Eat This Crapola Because They're Paying Me," had been a huge fucking success.

A lot of people ate fried chicken because of that ad. I saw a CDC report that said I was directly responsible for the average American adding thirteen pounds and two heart attacks that year.

After that, the sponsorships started flooding in, baby.

Ray-Ban paid me to pretend my advanced prototype Sony scopes were just normal sunglasses. *Cha-ching!* Hanes paid me to pretend I wear underwear. *Cha-ching!*

I got to star in a Ginsu knife infomercial and keep the knife, the matching carving fork, a set of six steak knives, *and* the spiral slicer when I was done. I got an official Dr Disrespect Chia Pet where you could grow your very own thick, green organic mullet and Slick Daddy on my terra-cotta head. I even got to meet the ShamWow guy.

CHA-CHING!

(And yeah, I know "cha-ching" was a thing like thirty years ago. But guess what? I just made it come back—*and* got paid for it.)

I was nineteen years old, and I was officially "rich as hell." Seriously, that was my bracket in TurboTax.

I lived in a massive top secret gated estate with mango trees and white tigers and croquet and all this other rich-person shit I didn't care about. I let Razor Frank stay in my guesthouse and earn money as my butler sometimes, just to pay him back for all those free meals he gave me when I was still poor.*

I ate whatever I wanted, whenever I wanted. So, Mr. T cereal for every meal. I owned a dozen Lambos, all blacked out. And tech? Bro, I owned the latest Samsung LaserDisc before Samsung did. Apple came to *me* for the very first iPod playlist (all Bell Biv DeVoe,

---

* I think he actually spoke English in this dimension, but I was so busy being rich I never really listened to what he said.

all the time). And Gateway—I told them to make all their boxes look like cows as a gag, and they actually did it.

I was the most successful, most dominant gaming champion in the country. I'd laid waste to *all* my rivals—not like you could really call them rivals. I'd embarrassed them in front of their mothers, humiliated them in front of their wives, but I pretty much made them look okay in front of their kids, because that's crossing a line.

But it was too much of a good thing!

I thrive off competition, all right? I feed off it! It lifts me to the peaks of the highest mountains, and I seek it out at the ends of the longest, darkest alleyways. Competition, danger, violence—it's what makes me who I am, it's what makes the Two-Time the greatest of *all* time.

All that was gone, and I felt like I had nothing left to prove.

So now, instead of celebrating the utter annihilation of my foes in *Halo*, instead of pumping my massive fist and whipping my stunning mullet through the air and screaming "YAYAYAYA!" at the top of my lungs—for the first time in my life I was wondering if maybe, *just maybe*, I should retire from professional gaming.

Hold on—did you catch that? Because that was huge. Fucking HUGE.

But finally something was about to happen that not only would challenge me, it would change the course of world history.

I heard a window break! My reflexes sharp as the claws of a jungle cat, I spun and threw my bowie knife.

"AGHHHHHHH!"

There, in the shadows, cowering against the wall, was this little hunchbacked dude with big bulging eyes. My blade was jutting out of his shoulder and he was bleeding everywhere.

"Ow, that hurts!" he whined.

"Stop crying like a skinny punk baby," I said. "That's barely even a flesh wound."

To be fair, I'm pretty sure I severed an artery and he was bleeding out, but still—his mewling was totally annoying.

"Now, who are you and why did you break into my top secret lair?"

"I am merely a messenger, Dr Disrespect," he said as he slumped to the floor. "I broke in because you are known to be a man who appreciates danger and combat and your doorbell wasn't working."

"That's not a doorbell," I scoffed. "That's part of my advanced experimental Honeywell XP-7000 alarm system with laser-powered motion detectors and multisonic trip wires. Strange that nothing went off. I'll have to contact ADT."

"I need medical attention," he groaned. "I don't want to bleed out before I give you my message."

I tossed him a single Band-Aid. "Sorry," he grunted as he fumbled with it. "I always struggle with peeling the little white tabs off the sticky part on the back."

"Hurry up!" I growled.

He put the Band-Aid on top of the huge gash in his shoulder. Honestly, it didn't do much. If that blood ruined my black wall-to-wall carpeting, I was gonna be pissed.

"Dr Disrespect, it is my honor and privilege to bring to you a message from the most ancient, most infamous, most powerful multinational criminal organization in the world. An organization so diabolical, so vile, so devious, that the very mention of its name inspires terror in the hearts of all who hear it spoken aloud."

He paused for, like, dramatic effect or something.

"The name of that organization is . . . *the Brotherhood*."

I stared at him. "What? That's it?" I said.

"That's what?"

"Like, that's the name? The Brotherhood? It's not, like, the Brotherhood of Evil or the Brotherhood of Hellish Criminals or the Brotherhood of Venomous Battle Cobras? Or, I don't know, the Brotherhood of the Traveling Black-Leather Pants?"

"No!" he said. "It's just 'the Brotherhood.' That's it."

"That sounds hella friendly. I know a few brothers who live down the street—Tom, Jason, Tony. They're pretty nice guys, they have barbecues, put on game-watches . . ."

"The Brotherhood does not host game-watches!"

"Really? They might want to. Great way to meet people in the neighborhood. I mean, they usually ask you to bring something, beer or sporks, but I never remember."

"NO!" he said. "The Brotherhood does not want to make new friends! And if the Brotherhood was invited to a potluck, it most definitely would bring a keg!"

"Well," I said, "as long as it's not some microbrew bullshit."

"*But*," he said, "what the Brotherhood does do is put on the greatest, most elite, most cutthroat illegal video game tournament in the entire world . . . the Kumite Except for Video Games and Also It's Real. Otherwise known as 'KEFVGAAIR.'"

My eyes lit up like thunderbolts on Mount Olympus. Which no one saw behind my complimentary pair of Ray-Bans.

"Well fuck," I said. "Why didn't you say so?"

"To be fair, I tried, but—"

"I've heard rumors, of course. Who hasn't? Losers, that's who! But I never thought KEFVGAAIR was real."

"Oh, it's real, Doc. The last 'R' is for 'Real.'"

Guess what? The little hunchback dude had a PowerPoint with him to explain the whole thing. Set his portable projector up right on my onyx dining room table. He moved pretty well for a guy with a hunchback and a knife wound, and the image he projected was high-definition, must've been at least 5K PPI DLP LCD OPP. I was impressed.

"Eons ago," he began, "in the year 732, a great samurai warrior known as Takeo rose to power in Japan. He was a gifted warrior from a young age, trained in the art of the katana and winning forty duels by the age of twelve. He was ruthless, cunning, and he knew no fear. He killed other men in cold blood because it made him smile.

"But his true love was Sudoku. He was the world's first gamer."

On the wall flashed an image of Takeo. He wore elaborate lava-red samurai armor, his kabuto was adorned with mighty horns, and his face was hidden behind a vicious, demonic black menpo.

"Badass," I said. "But I bet that mask doesn't have any Sony technology."

"False," the hunchback said. "It had the latest prototype Ibuka Clan lacquer at the time."

He switched to the next slide, of the samurai Takeo playing Sudoku and looking really pissed.

"Seeking out new competition, Takeo traveled to Hong Kong and held the very first illegal competitive Sudoku tournament, inviting champions from all over the region to battle him. He named the tournament 'KEFVGAAIR'—which at that point stood for something completely different. We don't even know anymore."

He clicked to the next slide, a collage of various games and puzzles.

"Over the centuries, the games played at KEFVGAAIR evolved in technology and sophistication. Sudoku gave way to checkers. Checkers to chess. Chess to an early form of Trouble, with a prototype Pop-O-Matic Bubble. There were no electronics back then, of course, no flat-screens, no consoles, not even electricity, except when they rubbed their wool socks against rugs and shocked each other for sport."

"Makes sense," I grunted.

The next slide was an old-timey map with all these colorful arrows everywhere.

"And as its games evolved, the infamy of KEFVGAAIR spread—through the region, the continent, and eventually the world. Most people think Marco Polo traveled east for spices and silk, but really he wanted the Scrabble crown.

"Throughout history, the globe's most brilliant leaders, thinkers, and competitors learned of KEFVGAAIR and traveled to Hong Kong to test their skills and prove their worthiness at the highest level of gaming."

This slide was marble busts of Caesar, Moses, Lincoln, Genghis Khan, and Captain Kirk.

"Machiavelli refined his political philosophy playing Sorry at KEFVGAAIR. Napoleon played Risk and was never the same afterward. Alexander Hamilton invented hip-hop doing 'rhymes with' in a game of charades.

"And then in 1943," the hunchback said, "a revolution! The world's first computer, ENIAC. And with it, the world's first computer game."

A slide popped up of a computer the size of a four-bedroom house.

Next to it, on a field of black—a single green dot.

"The game was called *Dot*. Pretty much all you did was, like, move that dot around the screen. It was really slow, and it only moved, like, two or three inches, and it blinked sometimes. Every now and then it would just disappear for ten or twelve minutes, and we'd think it was broken, then it would pop up again and everyone would yell, 'DOT!' Come to think of it, I'm not even sure it was a game. But it was a massive hit!"

"Cool," I said. I was lying—it sucked.

"*Dot* begat *Pong. Pong* begat *Pole Position. Pole Position* begat *Donkey Kong.* Or maybe it was *Donkey Kong* that begat *Pole*—"

"I GET IT," I said.

"The second revolution came in 1988, with the premiere of Jean-Claude Van Damme's seminal martial arts and motion picture event, *Bloodsport.* Finally, after all those centuries, we had a backronym that fit KEFVGAAIR: Kumite Except for Video Games and Also It's Real. As I'm sure you know, because you're a grown man and you have the internet, the Kumite in *Bloodsport* was complete and total bullshit."

"Look," I said, "I know what it says on Wikipedia, but I still don't believe the Kumite is fake. I mean, Frank Dux, Chong Li, Ogre from *Revenge of the Nerds*—they're all personal friends of mine, or totally could be!"

The hunchback stood up as straight and tall as he could. That was still pretty crooked. Seriously, he was maybe four foot eleven, unless you count the extra four inches from his hump.

"All of this history has led to this moment," he said. "Here. Now. With you, Doc.

"All those centuries of gaming champions—of warriors!—

formed the powerful international criminal organization that is the Brotherhood. And now the Brotherhood is inviting you, the Two-Time, to compete at the highest level of gaming the world has to offer. To travel to Hong Kong to face off against the greatest, most elite competitors on the Earth, playing the newest, greatest innovation in video games: *Halo*.

"The winner gets a large chest full of ancient riches, gems, and gold doubloons that will instantly make him one of the wealthiest men alive. But more important than that, he will receive eternal honor, everlasting glory, and lifetime membership in the Brotherhood."

"And the losers?" I asked.

"They will all be killed," he said. "You must decide now, Doc."

"So let me get this straight," I said, scratching my perfectly square chin. "You want me to drop everything, leave behind my entire life, and go with you to Hong Kong on a moment's notice? You haven't even told me your name yet!"

"It's Carl."

I laughed long and hard. It was an evil, diabolical laugh. The laugh of a champion who has finally encountered a challenge worthy of his skill. It felt good.

"Well then, Carl," I said, "sign me the fuck up."

So yeah, I went with the guy. Twenty hours later, I was in the Brotherhood's AH-64 Apache attack chopper, staring out the window at the Hong Kong skyline.

"Down there," Carl the Hunchback said, pointing. "That is the location of KEFVGAAIR."

It was the middle of the night, but luckily I was wearing my advanced prototype Sony XL-9000 scopes with 3D night vision, so I could make out the entire complex in perfect detail.

"It just looks like some random-ass abandoned warehouse."

"Exactly!" he said. "Just as I promised—a top secret, maximum-security facility that lies at the heart of the Brotherhood's vast criminal enterprise, entirely invisible to the outside world!"

"Wait, that was serious?" I said. "I thought you were kidding! Why wouldn't I want the whole world to watch when I kick everyone's ass and look great doing it?"

"Well, um—"

"I figured you meant 'top secret maximum-security facility' in a cool way. Like—and this is just off the top of my head, I haven't even given this much thought—giant black steel walls and blood-red towers with mysterious sweeping klieg lights and maybe like an iron drawbridge with a giant eagle skull or something.

"And then around the perimeter you'd have armored ninjas and tanks and *Robocop* ED-209s patrolling everywhere, and then like a moat that's filled with acid and mutant crocodiles and genetically engineered super-piranhas where if they bite you, you don't just die, you also get all these little baby super-piranhas growing in your spleen, and when they hatch you start screaming in total agony as these killer fish with vicious teeth are just eating their way out of your spleen.

"And then near the moat and the drawbridge you've got these big poisonous iron stakes and at the ends of the stakes are a bunch of ragged, bloody, gory decapitated heads, and a huge flashing neon sign that says 'WARNING! ALL WHO ATTEMPT TO ENTER THE TOP SECRET KEFVGAAIR WILL DIE. Media, please see

Will Call for your official commemorative press passes.' You know, something awesome like that."

Carl the Hunchback looked at me for a minute.

"Uh-huh."

"Listen, Carl the Hunchback—do you mind if I call you that?"

"Yes."

"Sweet. So, Carl the Hunchback, once I win this thing—and I will win this thing—I'm gonna be making a lot of changes around here. I don't know what those changes will be, and I don't even know why I'll make them. Honestly, I don't know much about this place at all right now, because we haven't even landed yet. But I can tell you one thing. One of those changes will involve klieg lights and moats and genetically engineered super-piranhas and bloody, gory decapitated heads. And **if** you play your cards right, Carl the Hunchback, you can be on the right side of those changes, you know what I mean? But that's a very big 'if.' "

Moments later, we'd landed on the roof of that lame industrial warehouse, and Carl the Hunchback was leading me through a maze of equally lame hallways. No retina scans, no electronic keypads, not even a fucking Brinks security guard. I don't even think the drywall was finished.

We went through one twist and turn after another. It felt like we had been walking for hours—and like they could've at least sent a golf cart to pick me up?—when finally we came to a big set of double doors.

And what was on the other side of those doors—*that* was pretty fucking cool.

I mean, not as cool as super-piranhas and impaled heads. But still, pretty fucking cool.

Spread out below me was a massive arena, twice the size of a football stadium, like Jerry Jones would see the size of this place and shit himself.

It was teeming with tens of thousands of spectators, packed as tight as they could get, shoulder to shoulder, practically on top of each other—definitely a pre-COVID situation*—all of them standing, screaming, pumping their fists, waving around money to place their bets, and straight-up crackling with ENERGY and FIRE and POWER and THUNDER and SMOKE and ENERGY.

We're talking brown people, ochre people, taupe people, black people, white people, people from every country on the planet, sweating through their clothes and speaking every language you could imagine in a booming, echoing roar.

YAYAYAYA!

And I could see why they weren't worried about security outside—each one of these spectators inside was armed to the teeth. Switchblades, throwing stars, nunchaku, lasers, swords, scythes—seriously, who brings a scythe?—and every kind of gun. Depending on your POV, it was either the safest place in the world or the scariest.

And the Doctor doesn't do fear.

Carl the Hunchback led me down the longest, narrowest staircase I'd ever seen in my life. On each side of us, the hoodlums and riffraff screamed curses and threats.

"You'll never leave here alive, Two-Time!"

"We'll put your head on a pike!"

---

* Like I said, hopefully this ain't your dimension. But yeah—you're probably fucked.

"What kind of conditioner do you use? Your mullet is vivacious!"
I laughed. This was my kind of crowd.

We reached the central arena, a giant bloodstained platform surrounded by a chain-link fence and rusty barbed wire. Inside was the latest in gaming technology—plasmas even bigger than mine, Xboxes even more advanced than mine, the next, unreleased generation of *Halo*—how the fuck did they get that??—even more experimentally prototyped than mine.

Packed in the center of it all were the other competitors, must've been twenty or thirty of them from all over the world wearing their various indigenous garbs: lederhosen, babushkas, keffiyehs, sandals with socks. Who even knows what country that last dude was from—probably Kiribati or something.

And way up above us all, a towering, massive, five-hundred-foot HD pixel display so the entire arena could watch the action.

The lights dimmed and the crowd grew quieter—meaning they sounded like a slightly less deafening tsunami. Then I spotted this balcony high above the central stage, hidden mostly in shadows, except for the outline of a golden throne in the middle.

On that throne there was this figure, almost entirely invisible in the dark except for his two hands. Except instead of two hands he had one normal left hand, and his right hand was—get this—nothing but an Xbox controller at the end of a stumpy amputated wrist.

I know, right? Fucking crazy!

"That," Carl the Hunchback whispered, "is the mysterious leader of the Brotherhood, Lord Hannn."

"So, like, the same as the dude from Bruce Lee's *Enter the Dragon*?"

"No. This Hannn spells his name with three Ns. Very different!"

"Yeah, okay—hey, can we talk about that thing at the end of his right arm? Is that, like, an Xbox controller?"

"Yes, Lord Hannn takes gaming incredibly seriously. So he cut off his right hand and permanently replaced it with an Xbox controller."

"So . . . there's some kind of bionic circuitry that runs from the controller through his arm and into his brain or something so he can just think the inputs?"

"No, he still has to push all the buttons and everything. He pretty much just cut off his hand and added an Xbox controller."

"But, like, now he has to push all the buttons with just one hand?"

"Obviously."

"Is he at least, you know, left-handed?"

"No, he is right-handed. Why?"

"Bro, no one even LIKES the original Xbox controller! It's clunky and awkward with HORRIBLE game play! And now your supreme leader cuts off his good hand just so he can attach it to his bloody stump and awkwardly play Xbox with his off hand for the rest of his life? What if he wants to play on a PlayStation sometime? Or a GameCube? Or even an OG Atari 2600? Hell, what if he wants to write a simple letter with a pen and paper and decent handwriting! IT MAKES NO SENSE!!!"

"I'm not following. But quiet! He's going to speak!"

A big, booming voice echoed throughout the arena as the hands—or the one hand and the one Xbox controller—rose into the air.

"I wish to welcome you all—esteemed members of the Brotherhood, honored guests, cutthroat violent gangsters, and of course

our handpicked elite gaming champions from across the globe—
to this, the one thousand two hundred seventieth annual KEFV-
GAAIR!"

The crowd started chanting immediately.

"KEFVGAAIR! KEFVGAAIR! KEFVGAAIR!"

TBH, it sounded a lot like the Kumite chant in *Bloodsport*, except with a different word that was more awkward to pronounce.

"Every year for centuries," Hannn boomed, "the Brotherhood
has gathered here, in this nondescript, absolutely top secret, and
totally secure warehouse, to choose the world's greatest living
gamer! The level of competition here is unparalleled, the violence
is unmatched. The skill and dominance that this tournament has
witnessed over the millennia—nothing can compare!"

"KEFVGAAIR! KEFVGAAIR! KEFVGAAIR!"

"And yet I, Lord Hannn, truly believe that the competition
with us here today is the greatest we've ever had before. And I do
not just say that every single year. Unless I really mean it. Which
I always do."

"KEFVGAAIR! KEFVGAAIR! KEFVGAAIR!"

"Now I shall introduce the very best of this year's warriors,
taking special care to sincerely respect and appreciate the cultural
heritage of each of our international friends.

"With us from Sydney, the top gamer from the Land Down
Under, *Kangaroo Jack*!" This big-ass spotlight shined onto this
dude with sunburned skin, a leather hat, and a crocodile-teeth
necklace, who, to the surprise of no one, looked exactly like Crocodile Dundee.

"KANG-A-ROO! KANG-A-ROO! KANG-A-ROO!"

Kangaroo Jack looked royally pissed. "Hey!" he shouted. "No

one calls me 'Kangaroo Jack,' all right?? My name is Jack Hortly. None of this shit I'm wearing even belongs to me, they just fucking made me wear it. I've never killed a crocodile, I've never put a 'shrimp on the barbie,' and I don't say things like 'G'day, mate!' or 'That's not a knife, *that's* a knife!' I'm just a normal dude from Australia who loves playing video games."

The crowd went silent for a second.

"KANG-A-ROO! KANG-A-ROO! KANG-A-ROO!"

The spotlight shifted to the dude in the babushka. He was pale, massive, looked a ton like Drago from *Rocky IV*, and was dressed in a red boxing robe emblazoned with a hammer and sickle.

"With us from the heart of Siberia," Hannn announced, "winner of the 1999 Mother Russia Gaming Championship, Killer Commie Ivan!"

"KIL-LER COM-MIE! KIL-LER COM-MIE!"

"Hi, guys," Ivan said, raising his hand shyly. "Big fan of free markets actually."

"KIL-LER COM-MIE! KIL-LER COM-MIE!"

Hannn raised his controller-hand and pointed at the next competitor.

"And from Beijing, Mr. Miyagi Min-Zhong!"

"MI-YA-GI! MI-YA-GI! MI-YA-GI!"

A dude in a ninja outfit holding a folding fan, a carp streamer, and a paper umbrella stomped on the ground in fury.

"Seriously, people?? I'm from Beijing! Mr. Miyagi is Okinawan! This is the stupidest—"

"MI-YA-GI! MI-YA-GI! MI-YA-GI!"

After that came Pretty Boy Batista from Rio de Janeiro, who was actually horrible at soccer and the only ugly Brazilian I've ever seen, then Pepe le Phil from Paris, who hated berets and had never been rude in his life, and Just Plain Usman from Nigeria. They wisely didn't stereotype him or give him a nickname at all, but sadly he was the one in sandals and socks.

He kinda nodded at me. Hmm. Maybe he was a secret double agent making contact so we could hatch a diabolical scheme together later. Or maybe being nice is just a Nigerian cultural thing.

"And that," Hannn said, "concludes my introduction of the *best* of this year's gamers. The others are very good, of course, but not . . ."

I didn't even hear the rest of his pathetic words. Fire flashed in my crazed eyes—RAGE—venom pumped through my veins—MORE RAGE—violence crashed through every atom of my chiseled six-foot-eight frame—MORE MORE MORE RAGE!

"WHAT DID HE SAY ABOUT THE TWO-TIME?"

Carl the Hunchback tried to grab me—

"No, Doc! Don't!"

—but I pushed past him to the center of the arena, where I stood tall and proud and athletic, glaring up directly into Hannn's eyes. Or, you know, at least where I thought his eyes probably were, because he was still hidden in the shadows like a coward.

"LISTEN UP, HANNN!"

"What?" he roared. "Who dares interrupt the lord of the Brotherhood?"

"I not only dare," I snarled, "I *double-dog* dare! I don't know who you think you are, why you thought it was smart to cut off your good hand, or even where exactly your pupils are right now because it's pretty dark back there, but there's one thing I do know—and that's who *I* am.

"I am the greatest, most dominant gamer in the history of the universe. I am the undisputed Back-to-Back 1993–94 Blockbuster Video Game Champion. I am the eagle that soars to the peak of Mount Olympus and the tiger that tears out the throat of his enemies. I am the butt-naked Vaseline-covered missile that shoots down the waterslide and the guy who does the robot at senior prom and makes it look cool.

"And I *damn well* ain't one of the others who are just 'very good.'

"The name-ame-ame is Doctor-octor-octor Disrespect-ect-ect-ect."

The entire chaotic arena went silent—and I mean *silent*.

"Did—did you just add your own reverb effect with your mouth?" Hannn asked.

I grinned, my mighty mane of hair blowing dramatically in a mysterious wind. "You're goddamn right I did."

Oh man. That is such a perfect line to end part 1.

Seriously—chills right now. But yeah, now you're gonna have to wait for part 2 to see how it all ends. Suck it up, punks.

CHAPTER 10

THE ATHLETICISM—WOW!

Everyone knows I'm the most dominant, most transcendent gamer in the history of the universe. Everyone knows that my silky yet invincible mullet is a thousand subtle shades of stunning black-on-black-on-black. Everyone knows that Slick Daddy is not just the Ethiopian Poisonous Caterpillar but is also my best friend—and your worst nightmare.

But what everyone *doesn't* know is that I'm six foot eight, with a powerful, dynamic, muscular, athletic god-body, and I have a thirty-seven-inch vertical leap.

All right, you got me—everyone does know that. And they know it because I say it pretty much all the time.

Now, I know what you're thinking.

You're thinking, "Doc, you're the greatest gamer ever, but still—you're a gamer. You play video games for a living. Why do you care how tall you are? Why does it matter how high you jump? Why is it important that you're a perfect specimen of quasi-bionic, possibly superhuman athleticism?"

First off, it matters because it's true—I really truly am all those things.

I mean, maybe *you* want to live in some shitty dystopia of absolute relativism where objective facts like height and one-rep-max squat and vertical leap don't really matter. But not me, man.

Second, it's the experience.

I know in your simple, narrow mind gaming is a thing I *do*. Just some activity where I lean back in my advanced prototype Herman Miller KX-5000 office chair, stare at my experimental 7K seventy-inch Sony plasma-screen, and push buttons all day.

And yeah, that's pretty much what it is.

But no, I was fucking with you—that's not *at all* what it is.

Championship gaming is a mindset, bro. It's a mentality. It's a *way of life*.

It's about knowing, in the marrow of your bones, in the chambers of your heart and the fiery depths of your soul, that you—and only you—are the most dominant, most destructive, most unstoppable force known to man.

I have become danger. I have become death. I have become the terror of the shadows that haunts you in your nightmares and hides under your bed waiting to jump-scare you screaming, **"BAAAHA-HAHAGRRRAHH!"** when you least expect it.

When I kill you in a game—and I will—I'm not just beating you. I'm not just scoring points or winning bragging rights or adding another trophy to the mountain of trophies I already have. I'm demoralizing you. I'm destroying your social confidence. I'm taking your very essence and offering your pixelated blood to the Blood God. I am taking everything you are and everything you had hoped to be.

That is what being a championship gamer means.

Now, I ask you—could I be all those things, could I have that killer spirit and devotion to pure berserker dominance, if I was fucking six foot two??

Could I embrace the champion's way of life if my body was anything less than the perfectly chiseled, diamond-cut, forged-in-the-eternal-fires-of-Mount-Doom athletic phenomenon it is?

Could I be the one-and-only Dr Disrespect if my vertical leap was only thirty-six inches?

The truth is so crystal clear I don't even know why we're talking about it. You *need* physical dominance to be a winner. You *need* incredible height and supercharged athleticism to be a champion. You *need* an insane vertical leap to snatch victory from the jaws of defeat.

In anything: video games, life, love, video games. Anything!

But I don't judge you for your ignorance. Just kidding—of course I judge you. But I *also* pity you. You simply can't understand how important in life it is to be physically superior to your fellow man—because, well, you're probably not.

Don't believe me?

Here's what I want you to do. Right now, I want you to get off your ass—no, don't put down the book, you gotta keep reading so I can order you around—and I want you to go look in the mirror. Yes, at yourself.

Now, we got two options here, right? Either a) you're a flabby, pear-shaped, cellulite-dimpled Grimace-body, or b) you're a skinny, stick-figure, stringy-muscled punk. Don't argue. You're definitely one of those two. That's just the way it is.

Now, the honest truth is that I, the Doc, the Two-Time himself, love you just the way you are. You go right ahead and be ridiculously out of shape. Have an ass the size of a semitruck. Have shoulders so bony they could cut glass. It seriously doesn't matter to me, because I'm rich and successful and inherently kind enough to love everyone, even you.

But after reading those straight-up *facts* about your body, how do you feel? Pretty shitty, right?

And trapped in that physical reality—a reality of being perpetually shorter, squatter, thinner or fatter, and less athletic than myself—you'll never have my powerful mentality. You'll never comprehend what it means to be a superstar hyper-dominant killing machine.

So what do we do about it?

Unfortunately for you, pretty much nothing.

I wish I could tell you that my physique is this impressive because I worked hard at it. Or even because I worked at all. I wish I could give you some list of turbocharged, foolproof exercises and dietary supplements that would magically transform you from a completely average, totally unimpressive human being into something Herculean.

But the reality is that all that garbage about the importance of working out and eating right and living a healthy lifestyle—it's all just a bunch of people trying to sell you shit you don't need and crap that won't work.

I was born this way, man. I'm incredibly in shape, but I've never worked out a day in my life.

I'm so fast, I could beat Usain Bolt in the forty-meter dash right now—RIGHT NOW—and I literally haven't stood up from my jet-black rich-Corinthian-leather couch in thirty days.

I'm so strong, I would dominate Dolph Lundgren in a steel-cage death match, even though I gotta admit *Red Scorpion* is way underrated.

And I'm six foot eight because, well, I'm six foot eight. I've never taken growth hormones. I've never even drunk a full glass of whole milk. As far as I'm concerned, calcium is for pussies.

I'm not gonna lie and say you can have any of these things, because you can't. It's just not in you. But I can help you fake it—at least for an afternoon.

How? Easy. Go RIGHT NOW to InterdimensionalChampionsClub.gg for your very own **DOMINEX, BY DOC** official athleticism-in-a-box kit. (Shit, isn't it fucking awesome not having Nigel the Editor around to fuck with my game when I'm trying to help my loyal fans—and earn a tiny bit of cheddar on the side?)

For the low, low price of $195.95, not including shipping and handling or an additional $59.95 I literally *just* decided to add to the price, you'll get delivered to your home address a large cardboard box that contains everything you need to pretend to be athletically superior like the Two-Time for a full afternoon, give or take.

Your completely non-customized **DOMINEX, BY DOC** will include:

- One **(1)** Pair of Adjustable Stilts and/or a Couple of Tin Cans You Can Strap to Your Feet (Six Foot Eight Maximum Height)
- One **(1)** Pair of Extra-Long Pants (Burlap)
- One **(1)** Pair of Attachable Turbo-Loaded Compound Springs That May or May Not Be Broken Slinkies
- One **(1)** Official **DOMINEX, BY DOC** Man Girdle, or "Mirdle"

- One **(1)** Advanced Prototype Foam-Rubber Muscleman Bodysuit
- That's Pretty Much It

Now, I know what you're thinking.

You're thinking, "Doc, that sounds like a pile of crap I could buy at any flea market for maybe a dollar seventy-five. What gives?"

And maybe you could.

Or *maybe*, just maybe, the fact that you're even thinking something that stupid shows just how *awful* your short, unathletic, tiny-vertical-leap mentality really is. Maybe you proved, right now, just how much you really need **DOMINEX, BY DOC**.

Because let me tell you what's gonna happen when you purchase **DOMINEX, BY DOC** and that carboard box full of shit arrives at your doorstep. Let me tell you what's gonna happen when you strap those adjustable six-foot-eight stilts onto your legs, when you put on that extra-long pair of pants and you attach those turbo-loaded compound springs to the bottom of your shoes. Let me tell you what's gonna happen when you buckle your fat ass into your Mirdle—and honestly, even if you're skinny, I highly recommend it, it's just that comfortable—and you zip yourself into your Advanced Prototype Foam-Rubber Muscleman Bodysuit.

First, you're gonna trip and fall on your face. Because honestly, getting the hang of stilts is harder than it looks.

But then, after you pick yourself up and wipe the blood off your lip, you're gonna walk out that door and for the very first time in your pathetic, pudgy and/or skinny life, you're gonna know what it feels like to be physically, athletically dominant over everyone else.

You're gonna stride down that sidewalk staring down at every man, woman, and child who passes by, and you're gonna think, "Hahaha, I'm taller than you." You'll marvel at how much smaller they seem from your tall-person's vantage point—like ants, really. Or losers.

You'll blink your eyes at the clouds swirling around your head at such a high altitude, you'll gaze at the mountaintops and catch your breath in the thinner air, and you'll think, "So this is what it means to transcend the pathetic limitations of short people."

You'll stare at these humans who are so much smaller than you, and you'll realize that they're not just little—they're also flabby and out of shape. With your stunning, molded physique, things you never even noticed before will suddenly really fucking piss you off.

The obvious love handles bubbling beneath some doofus's pink polo shirt. The subtle rounded slope of a coward's shoulders. The two-inch tribal tattoo encircling a weakling's pathetic arm. All of it will feel like an offense to nature, to perfection, and most important, to yourself.

You'll squeeze your firm foam-rubber biceps, you'll thump your fists against your carbon-reinforced artificial pecs, you'll caress the grooves of your square, plastic abdominal muscles, and you'll say to yourself, "Thank God I'm not those people."

And then, just when you think you can't feel more satisfied, just when you think you can't feel more like a winner, more like a *champion*, you'll see something in the distance.

Maybe it'll be a light post. Maybe it'll be a basketball hoop or a tall, rusty old sign at an abandoned gas station. Maybe it'll be a shiny red apple at the tippity-top of a tree.

Who knows what it'll be—I'm not a psychic—but whatever the hell it is, it'll be high up. Real high up. Way over your head. And you're gonna want to reach up and touch it.

But instead of looking at it and walking past with a loser's sigh like usual, for the first time ever, you're gonna stop and smile. You're gonna put your feet together—that's right, you won't even need a running start!—and you're gonna do a vertical leap.

And you're gonna snatch that apple, and you're gonna feel *damn* good about yourself.

And when you land back on the ground—only briefly, because athletic, jacked-up Adonises like you aren't destined to remain earthbound for long—you're gonna eyeball that high-up place you just reached and say, "Man, I bet that was a good ten feet in the air! Taking into consideration my above-average wingspan and superior height, I bet that was a thirty-seven-inch vertical leap!"

You'll be wrong. Because only the Two-Time has a thirty-seven-inch vertical, but still—it'll be an impressive vertical.

And for that hour or two, or at most a single afternoon, you, an average person, will finally know what it's like to be physically exceptional. For that small window of time, you'll understand what it means to have a champion's mindset.

The impact will be real, if short-lived. You'll get a raise at your job without doing an ounce of work. A pretty girl will smile at you. Your enemies will fear you. Your friends will respect you. You'll dunk a basketball.

Then it'll be over.

I know. You want it to go on forever, right? Or at least longer than an afternoon. But it can't, and it's for your own damn good.

Because the fact is, there's only so much physical perfection, only so much athletic power, only so many vertical leaping inches an average brain in an average body can handle.

Hit your mind with too much Doc too fast, and you'll go crazy! You'll be like the fucking Lawnmower Man.

You'll stare down at all the tiny people walking below you and start feeling dizzy. You'll touch your perfectly sculpted lats and your brain will glitch. You'll jump so high you'll burn your fingers on the sun.

So for your own safety, for your own sanity, once you've enjoyed your single afternoon of Doc-like physical superiority, I want you to take off your **DOMINEX, BY DOC** kit and destroy it. Or ship it back to me, at your own cost, so I can resell it to someone else.

It's enough that you've experienced, even briefly, what it feels like to exist in my perfect body. To know for a single afternoon what it means to think like a winner and live like a champion.

Savor that memory. Cling to it. And console yourself with the incredible gift I'm about to give you—part 2 of "The Kumite Except for Video Games and Also It's Real."

CHAPTER 11

THE KUMITE EXCEPT FOR VIDEO GAMES AND ALSO IT'S REAL

Part Two: The Champions Club, Baby!

All right, so in case you need a reminder—who are we kidding, *of course* you need a reminder—here goes:

I'd flown to Hong Kong to compete in the greatest, most ancient, most cutthroat video game tournament in the world, like this actual Kumite of video games called KEFVGAAIR. It was held by this shadowy, mysterious network of super-criminals called the Brotherhood—generic, I know—and I got pissed off, kinda lost my patience a little, which I do sometimes, so naturally I insulted their one-handed diabolical leader, Lord Hannn, in front of the entire arena.

Like, I called this loser out, okay? Totally showed him up.

So it was a few hours later, and I was feeling pretty good about myself, because I'd really made a great first impression. My guide, Carl the Hunchback, was showing me to my luxury suite, and suddenly I spotted the Nigerian champion, Just Plain Usman, gesturing at me through the cracked door of a secret double-agent spy room.

Or maybe it was just a janitor's closet. I had to find out.

"Um, you go on without me, Carl the Hunchback," I said. "I'll catch up to you in a sec. I've got to, uh, look at . . . something . . . around . . . here."

He rolled his eyes and kept walking.

"All right, Just Plain Usman," I said. "I'm getting, like, strong secret double-agent spy vibes from you. So what's the deal, man? And why the *hell* are you wearing sandals with socks?"

"Doc," he said, "I'm part of a secret international organization of double-agent hero spies that's been trying to infiltrate the Brotherhood for centuries. The earliest known socks, dating from 300 AD, were excavated from Oxyrhynchus and had a split toe designed for sandals. Socks were *invented* for sandals—why are you wearing socks without sandals?"

"All right," I said, "what's your organization called?"

"Well," Just Plain Usman said, clearing his throat, "we're also called the Brotherhood."

"JESUS CHRIST!" I shouted. "What is wrong with all you secret international organizations? Is it that hard to come up with an awesome name?"

"Look," he sighed. "I've been trying to get it changed ever since I became a member, okay? But there's a lot of red tape in these secret international organizations! It takes five meetings just to agree on an agenda, our Slack channel is an absolute mess. I've had to refile my proposal for our new name five separate times, in triplicate, but the registrar keeps losing the documentation . . ."

"So what is it?" I said. "Your pitch for the new name?"

"The Other Brotherhood."

"Yeah," I said. "BEFORE I STAB MYSELF IN THE FUCKING EYEBALL OUT OF FRUSTRATION, we're gonna have to move on."

"We've learned that Hannn uses the KEFVGAAIR tournament as a front for his entire criminal operation—illegal gambling, money laundering, grand theft auto, murder, extortion, international arms dealing, violence, and mayhem."

"Yeah," I said, "I mean, I already knew they were criminals, so . . ."

"But," he sputtered, "did you know how bad the crimes were?? The murder! The mayhem!"

"Yeah, gotta be honest with you, that all sounds pretty cool to me."

"But—"

"You literally just listed my favorite things."

"But—"

"Like a real-life version of James Bond meets *Goodfellas* meets all the *Fast and Furious* movies except *Tokyo Drift*."

"*But*—"

Too late. I'd already closed the secret double-agent spy room/ janitor closet door behind me.

"Hey, Carl the Hunchback!" I shouted as I jogged to catch up to my guide. "Hey, what kinds of crimes do you guys do, anyway?"

He shrugged as he unlocked the door to my suite. "Just the cool ones: illegal gambling, murder, extortion, international arms deals . . ."

"Sweet. That's what I figured."

I walked into the suite, and even *I* was impressed. We're talking a state-of-the-art flat-screen TV so huge, so massive, and so flat that it covered one whole wall. We're talking top-of-the-line speakers so gigantic they covered two more walls. We're talking a bed so fucking big and luxurious it covered another wall. Yeah, it was a Murphy bed, but it was a really awesome one.

And all the other walls? We're talking wall-to-wall-to-wall slate-black slate everywhere. That's a lot of walls, a lot of black, and a lot of slate. Plus one big-ass mirror on the ceiling.

That's my kind of room.

"Whoa!" I shouted as I ran over to the gigantic Murphy bed. I pushed a shiny silver button and it lowered from the wall automatically. Pretty fucking cool. "This must be, like, an experimental prototype Murphy bed, right?"

"Sure," he said. "Doc, I shall leave you now. You'll need your rest for tomorrow's KEFVGAAIR. I do not think Lord Hannn will easily forget today's . . . interruption."

"It's cool." I grinned. "I'll dominate."

Carl the Hunchback bowed and closed the door behind him.

I kept pressing on the silver button over and over again—it was so much fun watching the Murphy bed go up and down!—until suddenly the damn thing broke. Instead of going down, it slid to the side, revealing the entrance to a big-ass secret industrial warehouse.

And stacks and stacks of illegal merchandise.

Crates full of Kalashnikovs and M203 grenade launchers. Piles of rigged slot machines and roulette tables. Rows of Lambos and Ferraris and Jaguars with fresh coats of paint and filed-off VINs. And bale upon bale of counterfeit currency.

I mean, what can I say?

FUCKING AWESOME!

Then I saw something else.

Hidden behind boxes of throwing stars, a totally different kind of illegal merchandise. Thousands of small, lifelike plastic action figures. Each with its own blood-red tactical jacket. Each with its own pair of mirrored Sony prototype specs. Each with its own perfectly square jaw and flowing black-diamond mullet and little mini Slick Daddy.

That's right. The illegal merchandise was me.

Unauthorized, knockoff, bootlegged Dr Disrespect action figures to be trafficked in black-market toy stores in every country on the planet.

I picked one up. It was an awesome idea, but the workmanship was shoddy. The paint was scratched, my little mane of hair had no luster, and the Ethiopian Poisonous Caterpillar looked like it had retreated into a cocoon. And yeah, I just came up with that metaphor *right now*.

Worst of all—like worse than anything I could possibly imagine, including death by super-piranha—the Brotherhood planned to sell them all without giving me a cut. Not one thin dime.

I know this because they'd foolishly left their illegal global marketing and distribution plan on one of the boxes, an informative PowerPoint titled "Selling Our Bootleg Dr Disrespect Dolls to Millions Without Paying Him One Thin Dime!"

Wait a second.

DOLLS???

DR DISRESPECT COULD **NEVER** BE A <u>DOLL</u>! HE COULD ONLY BE AN <u>ACTION FIGURE</u> WITH MAXIMUM VIOLENCE—**WOW**—MAXIMUM SPEED—**WOW**—AND MAXIMUM MOMENTUM—**WOW!!!**

Yeah. That doll thing was officially the worst part of all, and my mission was now crystal clear:

I was gonna take down the Brotherhood, baby.

———

The next morning I strode to the entrance of the mighty KEFV-GAAIR arena of combat. The air was hot with thunder and smoke. The walls were shaking with the vibrations of thousands of screaming fans. Just Plain Usman walked up.

"By the way," I growled. "I'm in."

You shoulda seen the look on his face—he totally didn't see that coming.

"You're in!?" he whispered. "Excellent! If we attack as soon as we reach the stage, we can—"

I laughed long and hard.

"*First*, I'm winning KEFVGAAIR," I said. "*Then*, we take out the Brotherhood."

And so the tournament began.

Obviously such an elite level of incendiary competition can only be captured by a badass Jerry Bruckheimer–esque *Rocky IV*–style action MONTAGE.

I recommend listening to "Poison" by Bell Biv DeVoe, pretty much anything by Peter Cetera from the eighties, or the now-classic "Doc Theme Song" while you read the following bullets, for dramatic effect. Deejay, give the readers a helping hand.

Bump-tsshhh.

Bump-tsshhh-tsshhh.

"*They call him Doc!*"

- The Two-Time enters the ring in super-intense slo-mo. So damn slow and so damn mo you can barely tell I'm moving. Except I am. Oh yeah, I am.
- I gaze around the arena, taking it all in. The thousands of fans. The smoke. The flashing camera bulbs. The occasional knife fight. More smoke. My competitors. More smoke. I lower my experimental Sony prototype shades in this super-cool, super-provocative way, just enough so you can see my gleaming brown eyes—and the crowd explodes!
- **"KEFVGAAIR! KEFVGAAIR! KEFVGAAIR!"**
- I turn and stare defiantly at Lord Hannn on his shadowy throne. I point to where I think his eyes might be, then I make a throat-slashing motion across my neck. Then I point at his stupid Xbox-controller hand, and I shake my head and make the jerk-off motion, like "You're a stupid idiot," and also "Honestly, how do you even jerk off with that thing?"
- Quick shot of Carl the Hunchback looking totally terrified on my behalf, like "Oh no he didn't!" except not as blatantly dated as that expression.
- The scoreboard lights up above us, with all the competitors' names in fiery red neon.
- Sweeping scan of the dozens of elite international opponents in their caricatures of ethnic garb—kilts and bagpipes, kimono robes, giant sombreros, berets and baguettes, khaki pants and Sperry Top-Siders. They look awkward—and bloodthirsty.
- **"KEFVGAAIR! KEFVGAAIR! KEFVGAAIR!"**
- The rounds tick off on the scoreboard—*Round One . . . Round Two . . . Round Three*—as my reign of dominance begins.

- Shots of me pumping my fist, flashing the "I'm number one" sign, and screaming "Yayayaya!" as my competitors howl in impotent rage and spew all these hilariously stereotyped one-liners, like Kangaroo Jack screams, "Did you hear the thunder? I better run, I better take cover!" and Killer Commie Ivan shouts, "Better Red than dead! Pro gamers of the world unite!"

- A quick shot of Lord Hannn pounding his Xbox-controller fist in anger. Back in my corner, Carl the Hunchback strokes his chin, like "You know what? I think the kid's got it!"

- Shot of me doing a super-badass karate kick in the air for no good reason.

- **"KEFVGAAIR! KEFVGAAIR! KEFVGAAIR!"**

- *Final Round!* It's just me and Mr. Miyagi Min-Zhong. Mano a mano. Competitor versus competitor. I look him in the eye and nod. Finally a worthy opponent. This is it. The battle we've all been waiting for.

- Yeah, I kick his ass. Like, I beat the guy in maybe five minutes, a new KEFVGAAIR record. After it's over, I give him a firm handshake, because when it's all said and done, he was a worthy competitor.

- Then I lean in and go, "Hey, Min-Zhong, I just want you to know that I value your culture. The idea that they'd conflate a Chinese national with Mr. Miyagi is offensive and reprehensible, especially when everyone knows that Mr. Miyagi was born in Okinawa, Japan, where he was betrayed by his best friend, Sato, and then immigrated to California, where he suffered in an unjust internment camp for Japanese-Americans before bravely serving for the United States in World War II and earning the Medal of Honor. He was a patriot, a karate master, and a proud Japanese-American. He was not a cartoon and neither are you. That said, that whole thing where he tried to catch a fly with chopsticks was pretty dope."

- Then Min-Zhong goes, "Agreed."
- A furious Lord Hannn overturns a random table. It takes him a few tries with that whole missing-hand deal, but he eventually gets it.
- Final epic sweeping wide shot as I turn to the massive, roaring crowd and raise my fists in the air. They scream louder than they've ever screamed anything in their lives:

"DOC! DOC! DOC!"

My theme song ends with this one undeniable eternal truth:

"The name issssssssss Dr Disrespect!"

Followed by this totally awesome guitar solo by Slash from Guns N' Roses. Then—look at that!!—Slash is actually *there*, in the arena, jamming in the crowd as knife fights break out all around him and everyone holds up their lighter and waves them in the air.

And I'm rocking out with my air guitar in the middle of it all, soaking in all the glory, and yeah, all right, so maybe it's all a little over-the-top, maybe it's all like way, way, way too much, but you know what? I'm the world fucking champ, and this is my fucking blockbuster movie montage, so I'll make it as "too much" as I god-damn want.

"STOP! I COMMAND YOU!"

Still cloaked in shadows, sitting high on his balcony on his golden throne, Lord Hannn ruined the moment with his stupid shouting. I waved for quiet from my thousands of adoring fans.

"Listen up, Hannn," I said, all calm and arrogant. "I dominated your ancient mysterious gaming tournament exactly like I said I would. Fair is fair, dude—hand over my winnings."

He gestured behind him, and a flunky wheeled out this massive wooden chest and popped it open. That baby was full of diamonds, rubies, emeralds, gold bars, the works. This was like Jeff Bezos rich—*before* his divorce settlement.

"Fine," he said. "But you'll have to beat *me* first."

I grinned. "Your funeral."

The crowd—*my* crowd—went ballistic.

"DOC! DOC! DOC!"

"Doc!" Just Plain Usman said. "We gotta get going, man! I got the elite squad of commandos from the Other Brotherhood set to storm the compound in three minutes!"

"Call 'em off," I said. "I destroy vicious international criminal organizations on my *own* time."

I walked toward the console. Carl the Hunchback was giving me this weird look, like maybe there was a surprise plot twist coming up, but I shrugged it off.

"Let's do this, Hannn!"

The game started. And I gotta admit, I thought Hannn's whole "I'm gonna cut off my good right hand and replace it with a damn Xbox controller" thing was dumb as hell, but guess what?

It fucking worked!

That dude's left hand moved like nothing I've ever seen. He was using one finger to jump, another finger to crouch. One finger to fire, another finger to reload. One finger to throw grenades, another finger to switch weapons, another finger to move, and another finger to zoom.

I mean, how many fingers did this motherfucker have? Looked like ten, twenty, thirty, plus maybe a dozen thumbs, all moving in a blur, hitting one button after another, jumping all over that stupid Xbox-controller implant.

And he was playing on the big dog, the original Duke controller! So his fingers had a lot of ground to cover, and they weren't even *long*! They were these little fat, ugly, stumpy things. Like, not attractive fingers at all. That made it even harder to watch.

Now, everyone knows that I hate using controllers in general—tell me to use a controller instead of my mouse and keyboard on my stream and I will never speak to you ever again. Like, that's it. Mom, you're cut off. Dad, you're getting nothing in the will. You're dead to me. That's how seriously I take that shit.

But back at the 2001 KEFVGAAIR, using that first-generation prototype advanced Xbox console, playing with a controller was the only option.

You know what?

Didn't fucking matter.

Why? I'm glad you asked. Not really, because you should've known the answer. And the answer is that I'm the best. It doesn't matter what game, what console, what computer, or what controller. I cannot and will not be beaten. It's that simple.

So when I saw how Hannn could move, how he could work that ridiculous Xbox controller implanted on his right stump using his left hand, I didn't sweat it at all. I mean literally not one single molecule of sweat came out of my perfectly formed pores on my stunning alabaster forehead.

I just smiled and I started moving even faster.

Because a true champion doesn't quake at the first sign of real competition. A true warrior doesn't tremble when he's finally challenged. The Two-Time, Back-to-Back 1993–94 Blockbuster Video Game Champion doesn't run from the danger at the end of that long, dark alleyway.

No, he keeps right on running. He embraces the danger. He thrives off the challenge. He grows stronger from the competition.

This was what I'd been craving back in my lair. This was what I had missed. This was the VIOLENCE, the SPEED, the MOMENTUM I had been yearning for.

Now I'd found it. And I loved it.

My reflexes got sharper. My fingers and thumbs moved faster. My killer instinct became more lethal and more instinctual. I was the claws of the hawk. I was the fangs of the cobra. I was the wolf's cunning and the lion's roar.

And then something weird happened. As I steadily gained the upper hand—pun 1,000 percent intended—on Hannn, thin wisps of smoke slowly started emanating from his shadowy throne, from right around where his nose would've been if I'd ever seen it. Blood-red sparks started flying everywhere as an electric crackling sound echoed from his balcony.

CRACKLE-ZIIIPPP-POWWWW-TWANNG!

I had to get to that balcony.

From the arena's platform, I leapt into the stands. The rabble scrabbled. A few asked for my autograph, a couple more asked me to lay on hands.

I couldn't blame them, but I had work to do.

I jumped over four rows, then another four, then another four, because I'm just that tall and athletic.

I reached the bottom of Hannn's mysterious balcony and I

peered upward. The stream of smoke was getting thicker, the sparks had turned into a full-on blaze, the crackling and zipping were deafening, and below us people were running and screaming for their lives.

I've always been great at judging distances—just one of my innumerable talents, I guess—so I could tell that there were exactly 146 inches between the floor and the edge of the balcony. That's 12 feet and 2 inches. And that's a really long way.

For a normal man.

Thankfully, as you probably noticed, I am not that man.

Using my razor-sharp mind, I quickly did the math. I am six masculine feet and eight strapping inches tall. My pterodactyl-like wingspan is an incredible seven feet and three inches, and my standing reach is nine feet and one inch.

That meant that to grab the edge of the balcony and lift myself up to finally confront the evil Lord Hannn, I'd need a vertical leap of three feet and one inch—or exactly thirty-seven inches.

Are you with me? I know—you didn't think you'd get a math test in the middle of a high-intensity kick-ass action scene. But excellence is earned!

Now, I'd jumped pretty high before. Once I'd been trying to swat a mosquito in my Top Secret Command Center, and I'd jumped thirty-two inches. Then another time I was walking up some stairs, lifted up my foot, and BAM—jumped thirty-three inches, just like that.

But that was just me fucking around.

To jump a full **thirty-seven inches**? In a high-pressure situation, with thousands of people staring and a fire blazing and knives and throwing stars flying through the air and the fate of a global criminal organization resting on my next move—that's a big-ass jump!

For a normal man.

I crouched down, felt that elastic stretch in my calves, the burn in my thighs, and the atomic critical mass in my glutes, and I sprang into the air . . .

A Short Break

Can we just stop for a moment and truly appreciate just how many inches are in thirty-seven inches?

That's not one inch. That's not two inches. That's not three inches. That's not four inches. That's not five inches . . .

Well, you get the idea.

But in case you don't, that's also not six inches. It's not seven inches. It's not eight inches. It's not nine inches. It's not ten inches. It's not eleven inches. It's not twelve inches. It's not thirteen inches. It's not fourteen inches. It's not fifteen inches. It's not sixteen inches. It's not seventeen inches. It's not eighteen inches. Did I mention it's not eighteen inches? Well, it's worth repeating, because eighteen inches is still definitely *not* the same as thirty-seven inches.

It's also not nineteen inches. It's not twenty inches. It's not twenty-one inches. It's not twenty-two inches. It's not twenty-three inches. It's not twenty-four inches. It's not twenty-five inches. It's not twenty-six inches. It's not twenty-seven inches. It's not twenty-eight inches. It's not twenty-nine inches. It's not thirty inches. It's not thirty-one inches. It's not thirty-two inches. It's not thirty-three inches. It's not thirty-three inches. (You still there? WAKE THE FUCK UP!) It's not thirty-four inches. It's not thirty-five inches. It's not thirty-six inches. It's not—whoops, almost screwed that up.

Because it's true: thirty-seven inches is, in fact, thirty-seven inches.

And that's how high I was about to jump. From a standing start. Not from a run, not from a trampoline, not from a basket toss. Just a straight-up vertical leap of thirty-seven mother-effing inches.

At least, according to my estimate.

We're Back, Baby!

Dude, I nailed it.

Grabbed the edge of the balcony, pulled myself up in the middle of that electric inferno, ran over to Hannn's shadowy throne, and finally saw what deep down I'd known all along—Lord Hannn was nothing but an advanced prototype AI Sony Intel-Inside™ Hyper-Core i27-530000K 40-thread 11.9 GHz quantum-processor robot.

That's right. He was a fucking computer.

A really cool one, but still. A computer.

I reached back into the shadows with my mighty hands, grabbed all Hannn's computerized guts, and yanked them out of the wall. It was pretty fucking awesome too, because it wasn't just wires and shit—this was like *advanced* stuff, like Bishop-from-*Aliens* stuff, so there was all this green goo spitting out from all these tubes, and all these weird humanoid groaning sounds, and I could hear Hannn going, like, "Help me! I'm mellllting! Gurgle gurgle."

Yeah, honestly, if you ever get the chance to destroy a super-high-tech AI quasi-android, I totally recommend it.

So then of course—OF COURSE—the last thing I did was grab Hannn's stupid robotic Xbox-controller hand and tear it off of his robotic right-arm stump. I held it over my head like the greatest, most badass trophy I'd ever won—except for, obviously, my Blockbuster trophies—and I turned to face the massive crowd of Brotherhood hoodlums packing the arena. I screamed at the top of my lungs:

"LISTEN UP, BROTHERHOOD! I HEREBY LIBERATE YOU FROM YOUR EVIL ROBOT OVERLORD! YOU'RE FUCKING WELCOME!"

And I threw all that funky robotic shit, with all its clouds of smoke and weird green and pink goo and blood-red flames and smoke and MORE SMOKE, down into the deep, dark pit of the arena.

Then I paused, looked around, and realized I was completely surrounded on all sides by armed-to-the-teeth evil illegal gang members. I mean, these guys had guns, they had knives, they had swords, they had chainsaws, they had flamethrowers, they had surface-to-air missiles—kinda unsafe indoors, you guys—they had everything.

And leading them all was Carl the Hunchback.

"No!" I said. "You? Carl the Hunchback?? *You're* the *real* . . ."

A Short Break

Yeah, so I know this is, like, a pivotal moment and all, but have you gotten over just how impressive that thirty-seven-inch vertical leap was?

Wait—you have?

Well, whatever, man. I'm still super blown away by it. I mean, just—wow.

We're Back, Baby!

". . . leader of the Brotherhood??"

He smiled. "Didn't see that one coming, did you?"

"Well," I said, "I kinda did. There's always gotta be a twist, right? So, let's see. I'm guessing that you always knew I'd be the biggest threat to your global criminal organization, so you were like, 'Man, scoping out the Two-Time is a mission I can trust to no one else. I better go undercover myself, so I can, like, get close and betray him when he least expects it!'"

"NO!" Carl the Hunchback shouted. "That was not my reasoning. I just wanted a—a change of pace!"

"Uh-huh, right," I said. "And then I'm guessing that you hid the secret door in my room in the most obvious place possible, because you were like, 'Let's show Doc the truth about our evil diabolical plans to mass-produce a superhero action figure of him while calling it a doll—A DOLL!—so we can piss him off, and in his rage he will win the tournament, and then we can sell the action figure to children everywhere and make billions without giving him one thin dime.'"

"Um," Carl the Hunchback said, "you lost me there."

"You know what?" I said, really on a roll now. "I would bet my whole treasure chest of earnings—like seriously, no take-backs—that you're not even a real hunchback. You were just trying to throw me off the scent! Now you'll probably stand up straight and be like six foot two."

Carl the Hunchback looked at me.

"Right?" I said, kinda laughing. Dude kept staring, didn't say a word. Super awkward, which backfired and made me go all in.

"Come on," I said. "Like, no one's *really* a hunchback anymore, right? Modern medicine—it's the twenty-first century here. See a chiropractor, am I right or am I right?"

I looked at all the heavily armed criminals around him, hoping someone would throw me a bone. But they were all doing that thing where people won't look you in the eye and they pretend they're studying some speck of dirt on the ground while whistling nervously.

"DESTROY HIM!" Carl the Hunchback shouted.

So all at once, thousands upon thousands of these vicious, weaponized assassins all bum-rushed me, climbing over each other like army ants to get up to where I stood on Hannn's balcony. Thankfully none of them were superhuman like me, so they couldn't leap vertically a full thirty-seven inches . . .

A Short Break

WOW, right?

Just, wow!

We're Back, Baby!

. . . Then I climbed up on top of Hannn's broken golden throne, and I spotted Just Plain Usman kinda hanging out by himself down in the arena.

"Yo, JPU! Where the hell you been?"

He shrugged. "Enjoying the show."

I couldn't blame him. I do put on a great show.

"That's cool," I shouted. "How about you call in those commandos now?"

"I can't!" he shouted back. "You told me to send them home!"

Three gleaming throwing stars sliced through the air straight toward my head—

"Dude, I was kidding!"

—and I ducked at the last second. But shit was starting to get real, even for a hyper-athletic freak of nature like the Two-Time. Evil flunkies were closing in. Blades, bullets, and blood were everywhere, plus shouts and screams and fists and fury and violence, VIOLENCE, VIOLENCE!

I needed some backup, and fast. And it hit me—not the ten-millimeter bullet that whipped right by Slick Daddy, but an idea. I was already surrounded by the greatest champions the world had to offer. They just needed a leader. And guess what?

The Doctor is a born leader.

"Gaming champions of the universe!" I shouted from the top of the throne.

That got their attention. Kangaroo Jack, Killer Commie Ivan, Mr. Miyagi Min-Zhong, and all the other champions stopped what they were doing—which was mostly standing around shooting the shit—and they stared up at me.

"We came to KEFVGAAIR as rivals. We fought as enemies in this weird secret warehouse that didn't even have super-piranhas. And, surprising zero people here, I dominated every one of you. Like, it wasn't even close. I am actually embarrassed for you, your families, and the nations that you caricature—"

"Doc!" Just Plain Usman shouted. "You're losing the crowd!"

"But enough about that! Now I have a cause to bring us all together. Something so horrific, so evil, so diabolical, that no one can possibly stand for it. These BASTARDS, the motherfucking Brotherhood, are gonna sell cheap action figures of ME all over the WORLD without giving me one thin DIME! And they're calling it a DOLL!"

Crickets.

Seriously, never has an arena full of thousands of heavily armed criminals and champion gamers ever been so silent.

"*And* they also do all this illegal gambling and extortion and murder and arms dealing, and if I'm being fair probably some drug dealing on the side . . ."

Boom!

Mass chaos broke out. Kangaroo Jack pulled out a knife that looked just like Crocodile Dundee's. Killer Commie Ivan smashed a few vodka bottles to use as shivs. And Mr. Miyagi Min-Zhong assumed the deadly pose of the kicking crane.

"*YAYAYAYA!*"

From the top of Hannn's broken throne I flung my amazing body straight into the heart of the melee. With Just Plain Usman covering my back, I cut a bloody swath through Carl the Hunchback's gang of thousands.

Roundhouse kicks! Jujitsu guillotine chokeholds! Devastating headbutts without ever messing up my hair! And the speed of my blades—oh, the speed of my blades!

I whipped out new knives from every secret sheath on my body. And let me tell you—I have a lot of secret sheaths. They whirled through the air in a cloud of death, slicing throats, gouging eyeballs, never missing their marks.

Hundreds fell before me, but I had eyes for only one foe. The man who had betrayed me. The man who had turned out really to be a hunchback, which was awkward after I made such a scene about it, though I still have my suspicions. The man in charge of the entire Brotherhood.

"CARL THE HUNCHBACK! YOU'RE MINE!"

He sprinted through the arena—really more like a lurching shuffle. Gotta give him credit—if he was faking it, he was totally committed to the bit. And in the midst of all the death and destruction and piles of bloody bodies, he managed to make it to the roof. You knew there had to be a dramatic rooftop climax, didn't you?

I got there just as he was stepping onto his Apache chopper.

"You could've been a glorious commander in the Brotherhood, Doc!" he shouted as they lifted off. "But instead you've made a mortal enemy! Until we meet again!"

The Apache rose higher and higher into the dark Hong Kong sky. I had one last chance to get this prick—and one last hidden blade: my complimentary Ginsu knife.

How's that for a callback? Remember all those iconic infomercials I did, like two chapters ago? Now you know why you need to **PAY ATTENTION.**

My Ginsu flew through the air straight and true—so much better than a Miracle Blade—and caught Carl the Hunchback exactly where I wanted.

"Ahhh!" he shrieked. "My hump!"

The blow knocked him out of the copter and into the deep, dark depths of the South China Sea. All I could think was, "Huh, guess the fucker really did have a hunchback."

I turned around, and standing behind me, shoulder to shoulder, gazing at me in awe, were all the gaming champions of the world. It was a pretty badass scene—the entire secret warehouse in flames, the air smelling of burning corpses and Xboxes, the Apache falling out of the sky in a gigantic fireball—no idea why it blew up, but it did, so that was cool—and the screams of the Brotherhood hoodlums echoing below us as we sent them to hell.

It was so damn beautiful. If I wasn't so much man, I would've cried. But I am, so I didn't.

"I'll be the leader of my *own* global organization," I said, looking at the mighty gang of gaming warriors. "A brand-new organization of pure awesomeness. An organization that fights for violence, speed, momentum, and merchandise royalties for all! And we'll create the most elite competitive arena the world has ever known."

Just Plain Usman jumped up waving his hand. "Oh! Oh! Can we call it—"

"If you say anything that even *sounds* like 'the Brotherhood' . . . ," I growled.

He sat back down.

"Listen," I said. "I know exactly what we're going to call it. We're gonna be the Champions Club."

Everyone nodded, like "duh." Because obviously it was the coolest name for anything anyone had ever heard in their lives.

I had it all planned out, man. I was gonna take my new treasure and build a brand-new secret headquarters for my international club. It would have this sick-ass lounge, a secret lab, lockers for all the guys, and a trophy room that would only hold my trophies and no one else's, because, I mean, I was paying for everything. Oh! And my secret headquarters would have not one but TWO moats! And there wouldn't just be genetically enhanced super-piranhas,

I'd get mutant alligators and alien sharks and bionic electric eels too, and when I was bored I could watch them fight. Fuck yeah, that would be—

"Doc! Hey, Doc!" Just Plain Usman said.

"Dude," I said. "I was just having the best daydream about eels and piranhas fighting in my two moats. This thing where you interrupt me is getting really annoying."

"I was just wondering," he said. "You think we've seen the last of Carl the Hunchback and the Brotherhood?"

"Like, for the purposes of this book?"

"Uh, sure."

I laughed.

"Abso-fucking-lutely."

Because when does a vicious archenemy criminal mastermind who mysteriously falls to his doom ever make a surprise reappearance? Like, never—that's when.

CHAPTER 12

THE RIGHT FLIP PHONE FOR YOU

I hear it all the time. Like, constantly.

My millions of devoted fans see me walking down the street—or, I don't know, maybe I'm buying kielbasas at the grocery store or hunting down one of my mortal enemies, also at the grocery store—and they marvel at all my incredible, expensive, cutting-edge tech.

My prototype Google mirrored scopes with Sony 3D LCD night vision. My black-on-black Hellfire spec ops tactical vest with bulletproof, waterproof high-threat armor. My laceless Reebok Pump high-top combat boots with authentic XP-2000 pump action. My seventy-two-inch experimental AI Samsung LED flat-screen with quantum-computing 5K HD definition, which sometimes I carry around on my back just for fun. Or my portable 7T-43 laser-induced plasma-effect weapon with sonic boosters, which I stole from China and which can instantly target and hyper-vibrate your foe's spleen, eyeballs, and brain, and which I also sometimes carry around just for fun.

And they ask me, "Doc, what flip phone should I buy, and why?" Great question. And very, very complicated.

Sure, there's the technical stuff. The sound quality—that incredible tinny crispness you can get from the single monophonic speaker. The powerful graphics of the three-bit dot-matrix tricolor display. The seamless user interface of your twelve-button push pad: "Bro, do you see how fast I can toggle from J to L on this number 5?! I can send out a text every ten minutes!"

Some flip phones even have these plastic arrows you can use to move the cursor around. It's pretty fucking cool, but still kind of in beta mode, so not totally functional yet.

But if you've learned anything about the Doc so far—and let's be honest, you probably haven't, because you're not the sharpest shooter in the battle royale—you know that I always go beyond the surface. To an even deeper understanding of my own surface.

And the truth is that owning a flip phone is about more than just tech. It's about more than simple telecommunications. It's a way of life. It's a philosophy. It's making a statement—a statement that's usually kinda garbled, because you're talking on a flip phone.

When you're the greatest gaming champion the world has ever known, you don't fly with the bird crowds. You don't follow the herds of sheep as they *baaaa* and poop.

And what kind of phones do the sheep use? They use smartphones. More like stupid phones, am I right? I'm hilarious.

That's right. I see all you common people with your high-definition displays and your apps that can do a million helpful, useful, virtually essential things given our society's reliance on digital communication and high-speed computing.

And I laugh.

Yeah, so maybe you're able to order paper towels from all over the world at the touch of a screen. Maybe you're able to schedule a flight or check the latest scores or troll a gullible celeb on Twitter. Maybe you're able to find true love with a swipe up or down or whatever the hell direction it is. Maybe you're even able to take world-class photos and video using a wide variety of lenses and creative filters. You know, I've actually heard that some of those cameras are, like, professional grade, and TBH I could use something that really brings out the more subtle shades of black in my flowing black-on-black-on-black mullet, because my RED Digital Cinema 710-0322 camera with its Monstro 8K VV kit is fucking awesome but super heavy to lug around all the time, and—wait, where was I? Oh yeah.

But do you know how dumb you look with that "smart" phone?

Holding up this giant brick to your head whenever you want to talk. Carrying them around bulging from your pockets, totally ruining the aerodynamics of your pants. Dealing with all those accessories, your ridiculous PopSockets and screen protectors and rose-gold plastic cases. Staring glassy-eyed at your phone at all times of the day and night, when you're walking, when you're eating, when you're taking a shit or falling asleep—it's fucking obnoxious as hell! Unless you're staring at photos of me, in which case—all right, I get it.

But not the Two-Time.

My relationship with my flip phone is something deeper, okay? Something spiritual. Something self-actualizing on a whole new cosmic level.

The right flip phone in my hand is like an extension of my being. I hear it ring. And you know what that customized ringtone sounds like.

Bump-tsshhh.

Bump-tsshhh-tsshhh.

"They call him Doc!"

Oh yeah. I draw that baby out of my holster—of course I've got a holster—and I flip it open in one smooth motion. There's no fiddling with the password, no finicky fingerprint recognition, and there damn well ain't no fumbles or drops. Just one cool, well-oiled, slick—

FLIP!

And that baby is open for business. Check the caller ID real quick—I mean, my number is unlisted, obviously, but with fans as dedicated, as obsessed, and, between me and you, as straight-up crazy AF as mine, well, you just never know.

Then I lean back, bring that bad boy up to my ear, and the magic begins. Maybe I'm closing a $10 million deal. Maybe I'm insulting one of my countless mortal enemies. Maybe I'm yelling at Razor Frank to remember to do my laundry back at the Top Secret Command Center—*always separate blacks from darker blacks, Razor Frank!** Maybe it's just a robocall from Zimbabwe, but I'm playing it cool and talking anyway so no one knows I got punked.

Whatever it is, I look great doing it. I got that slim, aerodynamic baby nestled snug against my ear. Its slightly rounded edges contrast perfectly with my impressively square jaw. Its glossy black casing glints in the sun—or in the klieg lights of whatever exclusive red-carpet event I'm attending—and beautifully brings out the subtle shades of even darker, glossier black in my hair. As I move my supple, pouty, yet extraordinarily masculine lips, Slick Daddy dances and prances beneath my warrior's nose, and there's no

---

* In this dimension, *I'm* the one who speaks Chinese, and Razor Frank is the one who can't understand a word I'm saying. Boom! How's that for a twist?

clunky smartphone to detract from my flared nostrils, stunningly cubic chin, sheer splendor, or soul-stealing dominance.

My good looks get some breathing room—they can stop "doing" and simply *be*.

What's that saying? "If a flip phone rings in a forest and there's no one there to answer it, am I still a handsome bastard?" I'm no Zen expert, but that sounds about right.

And it goes without saying—but it bears repeating—that because I look great, I feel great. I mean, I always feel great, because I'm so successful. But I feel better than great. I feel bloodthirsty-killer great.

I'm looking good, I'm feeling good, and maybe, just maybe, I close that previously $10 million deal at *$100 million*. Maybe instead of an awesome witty comeback for my mortal enemy, I come up with a *mortal* witty comeback for my *awesome* enemy. Maybe I yell at Razor Frank to do both the laundry *and* the dishes. Maybe I'm extra charming on the robocall from Zimbabwe, and I make a brand-new robotic Zimbabwean *friend*. Hell, maybe we decide to grab a couple beers later that night.

And I'll be honest—sometimes using my flip phone is fun just because it pisses off the smartphone users so much.

"Okay, Doc, so I'll text you later."

"Yeah, sorry, man, have you tried texting on a flip phone? Not cool."

"Fine, then I'll send you a link to—"

"Hahahaha. A link? Have you *tried* using the internet on a flip phone?"

"No, but—"

"Like, I think this dot-matrix globe pops up on the little screen with the words 'World Wide Web' beneath it, and the globe kinda spins around for ten minutes, and it's not even smooth, it's really choppy, and then it stops, and it just says 'Error.' It's fucking hysterical."

"So you're saying . . ."

"Yep."

"I actually have to . . ."

"That's right."

"Talk? On the phone? With words?"

"Wow. You finally put it together."

"But I never do that! Not even with my parents!"

"I'm not your fucking parents. The name-ame-ame is Doctor-octor-octor Disrespect-ect-ect-ect."

"Why are you making that funny echo noise with your mouth?"

"I don't know what you're talking about."

So. If having the right flip phone is so critical on so many levels—technical, cosmetic, martial, philosophical—how do you choose the right one for you?

Damned if I know. I mean, seriously—I don't know you. I don't know what your face looks like, what your values are, what your income is, how much of a warrior you may or may not be. How the hell should I know the right flip phone for you? I'm not a psychic.

But I do know the right flip phones for me. Maybe that'll help you out, or maybe it won't—not my problem.

Motorola

As far as the Doctor is concerned, Motorolas are the crème de la crème of flip phones, to borrow from the Swahili. English can't capture how exceptional they are.

Who can forget the iconic Razr? No one with a combat knife in an ankle sheath, that's who.

And if you're like, "But, Doc, I'm only twelve years old, I wasn't even born when the Razor was around," then look it up, punk! Oh yeah, and when you Google—it's "Razr," no "O." No vowel at all between the "Z" and the "R." I have no idea why, but for some reason that makes the phone a ton cooler, all right? It's like someone took a razor to the word "razor," the ultimate conclusion of Occam's razr.

Once you do just a *minimum* of research you'll see just what made the Razr so damn unforgettable. Thin. Sleek. Shiny. Sharp.

I look at it and think, "Careful, Doc, you could cut yourself on that baby, it's so fucking sharp." Probably because I actually have cut myself on my Razr before, which might have to do with how surprisingly sensitive my perfect skin is.

Whatever it is, it's awesome, and it's Doc's choice of flip phone for when he's stepping out on the town and wants to make a call—*and* a great impression on the hundreds of paparazzi who follow him everywhere he goes.

Oh, and the keypad looks like something out of *Tron*. The original, badass *Tron*, not the bullshit sequel. So yeah, cool keypad too.

The Razr was, as everyone knows, followed by the Krzr. The Krzr was longer, narrower, and had exactly zero vowels. But honestly, it wasn't quite as cool as the Razr. Just trying a little too hard, you know?

Don't get me wrong, I still own seven Krzrs. I mean, I'm rich—so why not? And they're still pretty cool, just not as cool as the Razr. I own thirty of those. Each one is a different shade of black.

What's less well-known is that Motorola also developed a whole shit-ton of experimental next-generation Razr prototypes. Me being me, I own every single one of them. I use 'em depending on my mood or outfit on any given day.

Lazr: A black, one-of-a-kind, laser-powered flip phone that shoots actual lasers, and guess what? The laser beams are also black. Seriously, black laser beams! I don't even know how the fuck that's possible, but it is. This thing would've cost a normal person over $1.3 billion, but I won it in a game of *Street Fighter II* with Motorola's head engineer. Pretty sure I got him fired, but hey—no one forced him to play me. Anyway, I use my Lazr whenever I attend a movie premiere put on by my bud Chris Nolan, just to remind him I'm the bigger visionary.

Tazr: Specially made for cops, it can fire a charge of thirty thousand volts into a person of interest. I use this one when I feel like leaving my Kalashnikov and serrated bowie knife at the Top Secret Command Center and going less-than-lethal. So, I don't know, never?

Phazr: I got this one because I was like, "Whoa, I bet this is like a flip phone combined with a super–top secret *Star Trek* phaser weapon!" Turned out it was just preprogrammed with William Shatner's phone number. And you know what? Pretty nice guy!

Mazr: I pull this model out when I'm feeling trapped in a labyrinth of my own ennui or whenever I watch *Labyrinth*, the iconic 1986 film starring David Bowie's incredible Goblin King mullet. Slap that baby, make him free!

Blazr: I throw this one on when I need to look business-casual on short notice.

Hazr: This ultra-rare and ultra-expensive model is two prototype plastic cups connected by a prototype string. Part of me wonders if this is a joke at my expense.

But also, guess what?

The guys at Motorola were so blown away by my excellence, dominance, and success—plus the fact that I'm the only living person on this earth who still uses flip phones—that they actually created one just for me: the Dctr.

The Dctr flip phone isn't just a work of science. It's not just a work of art. It's on a whole other level, a spiritual revelation of portable telecommunications. Like, if Motorola had released this flip phone seven or eight years ago, they'd probably still be a real, authentic American company instead of just some bogus brand name owned by Lenovo. (To make my new customized flip phone, the entire original team behind the Razr came back together, led by the same head engineer I got fired years ago. Not like he had anything better to do.)

The Dctr is so thin I can slide it into my jet-black sealskin wallet and it makes less of a bulge than my black Amex. It's so sleek that if I could drive it, I'd take it over all fifty of my Lambos. It's so smooth that when I flip that baby open it almost disappears into thin air.

I'd say it's black-on-black-on-black, except there is no "on." It's a two-dimensional, highly glossed, highly polished black plane. No screen, no numbers, no perceivable interface at all. If I want a specific button, I just push . . . and it's there. Nothing but pure, strong, glossy black everywhere except for the cover, where, etched in a matte-black finish, is the silhouette of my flowing mullet, my cunning specs, and Slick Daddy.

And guess what? The Dctr can be yours, right now, at InterdimensionalChampionsClub.gg, for the incredible price of—

Nah. Just kidding. This one is all mine.

Nokia

I mean, what can I say? The Two-Time only accepts the best, and the best is Motorola.

But maybe for some weird reason you want . . . not-best?

Is there even a word in the English language for "not-best"? The very idea is so strange to my mind, so foreign to everything I stand for, that I seriously don't know. Oh wait. Waaaaait. I think I . . . Yep, that's it. That's the one: "loser."

So let's talk about Nokia.

In the battle for flip-phone supremacy, these guys are the only ones who even come close to the Motorola Razr. And by "close" I mean they're about five light-years away. Sure, they're reliable, they're stylish, and they've got reasonable prices. But they're number two. And because they're number two, they are, by definition, poop.

That's just a fact.

The only other fact you need to know about Nokia is that they're from Finland. Don't get me wrong, the Finns, the Swedes, the Nords, and all those really tall, pasty white people who eat lingonberries and meatballs—they're good at lots of shit.

Like vodka, shipbuilding, and berserking.

All right, I guess that's pretty much it. Oh, and making cheap furniture that ruins relationships. But the only *cool* thing they're good at is conquering Britain.

And you know what? That should be more than enough. You got your sacking, you got your pillaging, you got your big-ass helmets with horns and your god of thunder named Chris Hemsworth. Bro, you even got *Golden Axe*, one of the coolest classic arcade games ever!

We're talking sixteen bits of side-scrolling hand-to-hand combat. We're talking broadswords and battle-axes and an angry magical dwarf called Gilius Thunderhead. We're talking gaming history, gaming *lore*, that never would've existed without the Vikings.

And you know who developed *Golden Axe* for Sega? A dude named Makoto Uchida. One guess where he's from, and if you say Finland, I'm smiting your ass like Thor.

So I'm sorry—hahaha, no, I'm not—but the Nords were not put on this earth to make flip phones. They were put here to have big shaggy beards and to have cool names like Bjorn Irönside and Eric Bloodaxe.

And that brings us to . . .

Ericsson

Nords, come on, learn to quit while you're ahead! Fuck!

These dudes are Swedish.* And at one point, they'd actually made more flip phones than anyone else in the world.

And I know, because as the greatest international gamer of all time, I've been to every single country on the globe, no matter how mysterious, no matter how insular—just so I could say that I dominated there. Djibouti. Nauru. Kyrgyzstan. Texas. I'd touch down on some deserted field in my Kamov Ka-27 attack chopper, hop out with my Super Nintendo, find some local champ to destroy in *Mortal Kombat*, and fly away again. It was awesome.

---

* In two or three dimensions, Ericsson's mobile division was eventually bought out by Sony, and that's obviously not . . . Wait a second. What am I doing? Did you seriously buy this book for its *scholarship*? Get the fuck outta here.

Awesome, that is, except for one thing. Every human being in every one of these little cutthroat badass countries owned the exact same Ericsson flip phone, the T28. No joke. There are millions of them still floating around out there in the Earth's atmosphere. It's truly the people's phone, the ultimate equalizer. Cheap enough to be bought by anyone, anytime, anywhere.

WHO THE HELL wants a phone that literally everyone on the planet already has??

The purpose of a champion's life is to be *special*. It's to be *different*. It's to be *superior*.

It is *not* to have a knobby antenna and storage for 250 contacts.

Seriously, you can own a Nokia flip phone, and we can get along, all right? You can buy an old LG or a Samsung or even a fucking Alcatel flip phone—none of them remotely interesting enough for me to write about here—and I'll still have a *tiny* bit of respect for you. Like minuscule.

But if you own an Ericsson flip phone? Dude, you're not even dead to me. It's like you never even *existed*. Unless you find out my phone number, because to be fair, Ericssons do work pretty well and your calls will go through with no problem at all.

More Badass Tech Bonus Content

When the Two-Time is following his own path, when he's running against the crowd, blazing his own trail in the arena of technological combat, he doesn't just stop at flip phones.

Does the Doc ever stop at anything? Hell no.

So that means you're gonna get to find out about VCRs and some other cool shit too.

Betamax VCRs

Remember these incredible machines?

Of course you don't. You barely even know what a fucking DVD is. Well, look it the fuck up!

Back before Netflix, back before DVDs, even back before Blockbuster in all its VHS glory, there was Betamax. The original VCR tape. Smaller than the VHS tape, with longer potential runtimes and a higher-res image, the Betamax was superior to VHS in literally every way.

And it was made by Sony. Sony! The gods of tech! The same geniuses behind my experimental prototype night-vision scopes, not to mention the incredible Trinitron TV.

Yet the mighty Betamax got its ass kicked by VHS, becoming completely irrelevant a few short years after its release as VHS dominated the market.

Why? How the hell should I know? I'm not a historian.

But I keep an original Sony Betamax player in my top secret lab, right next to all my cutting-edge, advanced, multimillion-dollar audiovisual technology, to remind myself that if you let down your guard—even for a millisecond!—even the very best competitor can lose.

And also because I have a rare, first-edition original recording of Dolph Lundgren in *Masters of the Universe* on Betamax, which I watch every night before I go to bed.

Microwave Ovens

Fuck these newfangled microwave ovens with their digital displays and their rotating plates and their pussy-ass radiation-proof casing.

When I zap my frozen dinners, I want the complete classic all-American microwave experience. We're talking original 1947 Raytheons. We're talking six-foot-tall, seven-hundred-fifty-pound Cold War beasts. We're talking a cute little bell that dings when your leftover pork chops are still frozen solid, and lymph nodes the size of watermelons from all the gamma rays.

That's the experience I want when I'm microwaving my Orville Redenbacher popcorn for my nightly viewing of Dolph Lundgren in a blond wig and leather Speedos, all right?

Sony Discman

Now, I know what you're thinking.

You're thinking, "Doc, what about the Walkman? Isn't that more iconic, more retro, than the Discman?"

As usual, your question shows just how ignorant you really are. The point isn't to embrace shit that's iconic. And it damn well isn't about being "retro," whatever the hell that means. Do you see me lugging around an old Bell rotary phone wherever I go? Of course not!

The point is to be different! To go your own way!! And to look incredibly cool doing it!!!

Any dumb skinny punk hipster can walk around with a Walkman on his belt. And why not? They're the most revolutionary advance in portable audio of all time! They're small, they're lightweight, the sound quality is top-notch, they never skip or scratch, and you can drop those fuckers a thousand times and they still work. Also they're made by my boys at Sony, who totally deserve a win after all that Betamax bullshit.

But that is exactly the problem, man. It's *too* easy, *too* sensible, *too* accessible to be truly worthy of the Two-Time.

The Discman, on the other hand, is technology for the sheer sake of technology, advance for the sheer sake of advance. It's not nearly as reliable as the Walkman: It skips. The discs get scratched. The laser gets smudged. It breaks if you fucking sneeze on it (to be fair, I have a superhumanly powerful sneeze).

But man—it looks *so fucking cool*. It's sleek, it's smooth, it's all curves and beveled edges where the Walkman is a dumpy little box. It's powered by its own little internal mini-laser! Who cares how well it works?? And it's also made by Sony!

When I've got my original Discman strapped to my powerful thigh in the middle of my sixth set of twelve three-hundred-fifty-pound squats, I look fucking incredible, baby. So what if it skips every third note on my rare, first-edition original CD of the *Masters of the Universe* soundtrack, composed by the brilliant Bill Conti (*Rocky*, *The Karate Kid*, all the greats)?

Good looks, style, dominance, success, excellence, uniqueness—people, you gotta work for these things, you gotta sacrifice. Unless you're like me and you're just born that way. In either case, it's Discman all the way.

Nintendo Entertainment System

Remember all that stuff I said about how you gotta work and sacrifice for everything?

Yeah, well, sometimes rules are proved by exceptions.

The original NES is actually incredibly, ridiculously easy to buy.

Find that shit online and it can be yours in days, which makes it pretty ordinary. But you know what? It's worth breaking my champion's creed for one simple reason.

Mike Tyson's Punch-Out!!

I mean, look. I love multiplayer shooter games. Why shouldn't I? I dominate them. I got rich dominating them. I built an empire dominating them. Also, they're badass.

But there's simply no question that *Mike Tyson's Punch-Out!!* is the most awesome video game ever created. Period. We're talking fluid, intuitive, lightning-quick gameplay. We're talking graphics that are still fun and entertaining even by today's standards. We're talking top-notch iconic characters like Von Kaiser and Don Flamenco and Great Tiger and Soda Popinski, and the kind of hilarious unironic ethnic stereotypes you could only get away with in the late eighties. We're talking the poignant hard-knocks story of Little Mac and Doc Louis set to an electronic rendition of the song "Look Sharp/Be Sharp March" that still gives me a lump in my manly throat to this day. And most of all, we're talking the one, the only, Mike Tyson, the greatest heavyweight champion of all time, an almost impossible-to-beat boss—except for me—and a dude who in real life bit off Evander Holyfield's motherfucking ear on pay-per-view TV.

Did you hear that?

HE BIT OFF A MAN'S EAR IN REAL LIFE ON PAY-PER-VIEW.

Soda Popinski. Little Mac. Mike Tyson. Bitten-off prizefighter ears.

This is a game that is the purest incarnation of VIOLENCE…

of SPEED . . .

Of—

FUCK.

Holy shit, can you believe this? I haven't heard from Nigel the Editor in days—TBH, don't miss the guy at all—but now he's pinging me on AOL Instant Messenger.

Sorry, guys, this right here is an official . . .

Real-Time Update

Whoa whoa whoa.

All right, so this is definitely Nigel the Editor's AIM that's coming through—I mean, he's the only dude I know who uses AIM anymore, so that's no surprise—but something tells me this isn't actually Nigel the Editor . . .

It begins, *Doc—this is **not** Nigel the Editor.* See what I mean?

Wait, another AIM is coming through: *Stop writing your stupid book and pay attention.*

Wait, how does this mystery person know I'm writing a book? (And it is *not* stupid!)

It is absolutely a stupid book. And we know because we know all. We have ears everywhere. Eyes everywhere. Spies everywhere. We are . . . the Brotherhood.

The Brotherhood?! Oh shit!

Didn't see that one coming, did you?

I mean, if I'm being honest . . .

Bullshit. This was a total surprise and you know it!

Whatever you say, Carl the Hunchback.

But you saw me plummet to my doom in the icy depths of the ocean! And you KNOW that nickname is insensitive!

Dude, everyone knows that the evil archenemy who plummets to his doom isn't really dead. We all knew you were coming back. Like, all of us. And it's not my fault you have a hunchback. I mean, go to a fucking chiropractor or—

Enough! I've been waiting for this moment. My chance to get my vengeance for what you did to me, to the Brotherhood, to the ancient KEFVGAAIR tournament, and to our entire global criminal enterprise. I've been planning, plotting, scheming, then planning some more. And now, after all these years—

Yeah, yeah, we get it! I know what you're gonna say, all right, man? You kidnapped Nigel the Editor, and now you're using him as bait to lure me into combat so you can kill me and finally get your revenge blah blah blah.

Damn, was it really that obvious?

I mean, as soon as Nigel the Editor told me he was going on vacation to Hong Kong, I thought, "Shit, that stupid Brotherhood and Carl the Hunchback are gonna kidnap his ass and try to force me into some badass final showdown."

We told him he won an all-expenses-paid first-class trip! He fell for it completely!

I'll think about it.

What?

I said I'll think about it, all right? I've still got a ton of work to do on this book! Which is awesome and not stupid, BTW. I got all these deadlines coming up, and this new editor the publisher gave me—his name is Milton—is a real fucking ballbuster. And look, it's not like Nigel and I parted on the best terms, you know? All that shit he gave me about selling my merch and what I'm actually a doctor of and not writing a whole chapter that consisted only of the world's longest yayayayayayayay yayayayayayayayayayayayayaya yayayayayayayayayayaya—

For the love of God, stop!

But, you know, I guess I'll *consider* rescuing him?

But—but my revenge!

Like, maybe after I finish rocking out on this next chapter?

But—but he eats so much food!

Okayyyy . . . deleting AIM now, like I shoulda done ten years ago . . .

And he's so fucking annoying!

Later, Carl the Hunchback. I mean, maybe, maybe not—who knows?

CHAPTER 13

HOLLYWOOD DOMINATION— AND DOC'S DISILLUSIONMENT

Look, man. You know me. Hopefully not too well, because that would be creepy.

But still, you know that the Two-Time is never satisfied. So even after I assembled a Champions Club of the world's greatest gamers in the most elite arena of all time, even after I amassed a fortune in diamonds and gold doubloons and black-on-black Lamborghini Diablos, it took, I don't know, maybe a few months before I needed a new challenge. Or was it a few weeks? Or a few days? Who knows, it all gets a little blurry when you're so goddamn dominant.

But there was one thing I did know, and that was that I needed something new to dominate. Something fresh, something original.

Instead I got Hollywood.

But you know—beggars can't be choosers, right?

Hahaha, just kidding—I've never begged for anything in my life. NEVER! It's just a stupid expression I decided to use. And in this case, not only did I not beg—WHICH I'VE NEVER DONE, DON'T FORGET THAT!!—but I didn't even have to look very hard, because it landed right in my big-ass top secret backyard.

I'd just finished up my typical morning.

I'd street-raced one of my Diablos through the twists and turns of a nearby canyon, coming close to absolute destruction four times and laughing after every single one. I'd taken two multimillion-dollar business calls with industry titans on my flip phone. I'd polished both trophies from my back-to-back 1993–94 Blockbuster Video Game Championships, which took forty-seven minutes, and then I challenged—and beat—Razor Frank in hand-to-hand ninja combat, which only took six minutes.*

After that I'd returned to my studio, I'd started streaming, and I'd dominated *Call of Duty: Modern Warfare*. Racking up thousands of kills, leaving skinny punks dying in my wake, ruling with ferocity, terror, and intimidation.

All before 10:30 a.m. Just another day in the arena. Yawn.

So I decided to check out what was going on around my estate. Of course I had my walls and my moats and my gun turrets and my genetically engineered super-piranhas. But I also had an advanced experimental closed-circuit HD video system with audio capabilities deployed throughout the grounds of the Top Secret Command Center.

I could see everything. I could hear everything. I could guard

---

* In this dimension—and this dimension *only*—Razor Frank and I speak the same language, but we have no idea what it is.

against even the slightest intrusion by any of my thousands of bloodthirsty mortal enemies.

I could also spy on my neighbors, which helped pass the time when I was bored.

So I sat back in my custom-designed slate-black Corinthian-leather La-Z-Boy, turned on my digitally enhanced seventy-inch 4K Toshiba flat-screen security monitors, and took a peek at what was going on next door.

I gotta admit, it was a pretty classy joint. A giant mansion with wide green grounds, some big Greek columns, and a bunch of fountains with sculptures of Cupid pissing. Now, usually I would've just moved on to spying on my other rich neighbors, but this time I saw something different.

A big-time Hollywood shoot for a brand-new, big-budget TV show. We're talking ten luxurious trailers for the cast and crew. We're talking four 8K RED digital cameras, smoke machines, and pyrotechnics. We're talking hair, makeup, wardrobe, grips, dolly grips, gaffers, best boys, assistants to the producer's assistants, and all the other millions of mostly useless people you find on a set.

And there, right in the middle of it all, a state-of-the-art AH-64 Apache attack chopper, as black and merciless as death, its sleek metal frame gleaming like a knife edge in the sun.

That's right, when I looked closely I realized the new TV show wasn't a new show at all. It was a reboot of a classic. The most iconic, influential syndicated television program of all time.

Yeah. I'm talking about *Airwolf.*

I was intrigued. I grew up watching *Airwolf,* of course, because I have great taste. As a boy I'd been riveted by the awesome tech, blown away by the badass aerial battle scenes, and thunderstruck by the thespian science dropped by Ernest Borgnine and Jan-Michael Vincent.

I'd also been a little pissed off. Since I'd never met the creators of *Airwolf*, how had they managed to copy my look, my energy, my vibe so well? I mean, even at the age of five I was obviously cooler than Stringfellow Hawke—that's right, that's the main character's actual name. But still, they were totally ripping me off. Maybe I'd sue them once I hit puberty.

But life and world domination got in the way, so I never did.

Now, all these years later, maybe this was my chance to add my own legend to the *Airwolf* experience. To break into the A-list entertainment industry with all its trappings. Or at the very least to sue them into oblivion—because really, can you ever have too much money?

Maybe this was the new challenge I'd been looking for, or at least a decent way to kill an afternoon.

I zoomed in my security cameras on the production's call sheet to figure out all the deets. It was the shoot's very first day, and the stakes couldn't have been higher.

This was the biggest original web production in the history of Snapchat, and that includes *Bringing Up Bhabie*. The budget was over $20 million. It was starring megastar Mark-Paul Gosselaar as Stringfellow Hawke's wayward son, Hardtackle. And it was being directed by George Lukas. That's Lukas with a "K," so not the legend who created *Star Wars*—but this dude still looked pretty good.

They were gearing up for their first shot of the day. The first and the biggest—a stunt with that incredible, and incredibly expensive, Apache attack chopper.

I grinned and turned up my audio. This was gonna be fun.

"Hey, Neal," George Lukas called to the stunt pilot. "You sure you got this?"

Neal the Stunt Pilot approached the attack chopper, and any idiot could've spotted the hesitation in his step. He looked like a good kid, the kind of son who listened to his mommy, who ran home whenever she ding-a-linged the triangle at dinnertime.

But in his eyes you could see fear. He preferred the light places, the comfortable zones, out in the open with various people, laughing and frolicking and eating brunch. He avoided the long, dark alleyways, ran from danger, and hid from the chaos of battle.

So yeah, Neal the Stunt Pilot had no idea what the fuck he was doing.

"Um, sure, Mr. Lukas," he said with his voice cracking, like a soda jerk. "All good!"

"Okay, fantastic," George Lukas said. "So you'll be taking off nice and easy, nothing too complicated—then maneuvering past that radio tower, then dodging four drones as scorching pyrotechnics erupt all around you, then doing a straight nosedive at the cold, hard earth until you finally pull up at the last second without a scratch on you.

"Oh, and be careful around those drones, those are ridiculously expensive. But they're not nearly as pricey as the multimillion-dollar helicopter you're about to fly. Got it?"

Neal the Stunt Pilot gulped. "Totally."

George Lukas patted him on the back, then turned to his assistant as the pilot shuffled away.

"Hey," he said, "do you think we should've spent some more money on that stunt pilot?"

"Nah," the assistant said. "I found him on Craigslist. How bad could he be?"

"Shit," George Lukas said. "People still use Craigslist?"

The assistant shrugged. "At least one, apparently."

Neal the Stunt Pilot sat in the cockpit, about to head down that long, dark, winding alley of fear for the very first time in his life.

And I—denizen of destruction, cheater of death, master of basic helicopter safety—knew exactly what was going to happen.

Yep, just minutes after taking off, the damn thing crashed.

It was actually going pretty well at first. Then this crazed hawk came out of nowhere, forcing Neal the Stunt Pilot to swerve. The Apache collided violently with the drones, spinning out of control, plummeting out of the sky, and finally, in a giant ball of smoke and sparks and raging fire, exploding against one of those fountains with the pissing Cupids.

It was cool as fuck.

Thankfully, the crazed hawk was unharmed. Especially because it was *my* crazed hawk. I'd released the little bastard thirty seconds earlier from my own private aviary after telling him, "Hey, bro, let's make shit interesting. That's between me and you."

Oh yeah, I guess it was also good that Neal the Stunt Pilot was pretty much okay. Lucky for him, those Cupids he crashed into peed all over everything and helped put out the fire. So Neal the Stunt Pilot was basically unharmed except for the fourth-degree burns covering 60 percent of his body, a shattered femur, an obliterated spleen, and a left eyeball that was just kind of dangling out of the socket in this really gross but also totally awesome way.

Yeah, he'd probably never fly a helicopter again—he'd be lucky if he could ride a Rascal with those injuries. But let's be honest, the skies are much safer without him. He had no idea how to conquer his fear, no ability to embrace danger, to walk down that long, dark alleyway and never turn back.

And he also wasn't very good at dodging crazed hawks, but mostly his problem was fear.

"What are we gonna do now?" George Lukas shouted as the medics carted away the pathetic screaming stunt pilot. "We can't just call off the shoot! This is fucking *Airwolf*!"

His assistant sighed and shook his head. "Craigslist doesn't seem to have any other—"

"Wait!" George Lukas said. "What's that sound?"

A deep, steady rhythmic thumping echoed over the smoky field. It was the sound of ancient Native American warriors beating their sacred drums before battle. It was the sound of your enemy's heart, still beating after you tear it from his chest. It was the sound of Dr Disrespect piloting his own personal Russian Kamov Ka-27 Helix attack chopper.

I flew low over the horizon, parting the swirling clouds and landing just inches away from the Apache's wreckage. I was also blasting a favorite song from my prototype Bose XV-9000 sound system—

Bump-tsshhh.

Bump-tsshhh-tsshhh.

"They call him Doc!"

Because I know how to make an entrance.

"What the . . . ?" George Lukas said.

He and his assistant stared, stunned, their mouths open, their eyes wide. They looked like a couple of idiots. It was pretty funny.

My chopper's blades slowed. I stepped out as the smoke and flames of the wreck whirled around me, along with some extra smoke from the dry-ice machines I'd brought along. My frame was massive, my superiority obvious. My hair's black steel caught the light of the fire and my tactical goggles gleamed as I surveyed the destruction around me.

"Looks like you've had some helicopter problems," I said.

Fuck, what a line.

"That's my Kamov Ka-27," I continued, gesturing at my helicopter. "I had it custom-designed by the world's tippity-top engineers. All blacked out, of course. Your stock Apache is a decent chopper, nice range, solid maneuverability. But if I get in a dogfight up there, if it's just me and the enemy, one on one, staring each other down with blood in our eyes and hatred in our souls, I'm taking the Kamov every time. We're talking firepower, we're talking explosiveness. We're talking speed, violence, and momentum. And it's great at dodging crazed hawks."

George Lukas looked at me funny.

"Not that I would know anything about that," I said.

He stared at me for a long time. Like, it was getting super awkward.

Finally he spoke.

"Well," George Lukas said, "I think we found our stunt pilot."

I threw back my head and laughed loud and hard. And suddenly I stopped, looked at him, and said super-dramatically like a total badass:

"Stunt pilot? I don't think so. The Two-Time is nothing less than a star."

George Lukas arched his eyebrow, and the assistant blurted out,

"What?! Sir, no—you can't possibly make this random guy the lead of the show. Sure, he's got the presence of a modern-day black-ops Apollo, and his mustache is sublime, but our careers are riding on this, not to mention the entire reputation of Snapchat as a creator of groundbreaking dramatic television. We *cannot* make this no-name the star! What will I tell Mark-Paul Gosselaar? He's waiting in his trailer now, sipping a Coke Zero!"

George Lukas stared at me again, but not as long as the first time.

"We're doing this," he said quietly.

"But—"

"*We're doing this!*" he shouted. "I'll fire Mark-Paul Gosselaar myself if I have to! I don't know much in this world. I don't know a thing about cameras, sound, narrative structure, or television production. I have no *idea* how the hell I got this job, except maybe they got confused by my name.

"But," he said, pointing at me, "I know one thing. That man standing there is a star."

I smiled. Pointing is kind of rude, but I let it slide. "You made the right move, George Lukas," I said. "Probably your first right move since you killed off Jar-Jar Binks in *Episode II*."

"Um," he said, "I'm not—"

"Here," I said, tossing him a little piece of wadded-up paper. "I wrote down the number to my private flip phone. Direct line. Call me when you're ready to roll. I'll be up there in the clouds, blowing shit up, combing Slick Daddy before my close-up, and emailing your lawyers all of my ridiculous contract demands."

I turned and started climbing back into the cockpit of my Kamov Ka-27 Helix.

"Wait!" George Lukas shouted. "*Wait!*"

I paused, barely turning my head.

"Who—who the fuck are you?"

I pulled down my 3D prototype specs, and for the first time I looked him in the eye.

"The name-ame-ame is Doctor-octor-octor Disrespect-ect-ect-ect."

With the subtle wrigglings of a snake, I slid behind the control panel of my chopper.

George Lukas called after me, "Huh? I couldn't understand you with all that reverb! Wait—there's paperwork and W-9s and liability waivers! *Don't you want your script?*"

Details. Maybe important to lesser men, but not to me. As my Kamov Ka-27 rose into the hot, smoky air, one sound rang out above the rumble of the engines, the whir of the blades, and the thumping bass of my own blasting theme music:

"*Yayayaya!*"

———————

Anyway, I completely destroyed the shoot in two days.

Turned out these pussies wanted me to use *fake* ammo, *fake* air-to-surface missiles, *fake* cluster bombs, *fake* napalm—fake fake fake fake—for all my action scenes. I mean, the Doc doesn't fake anything, man. And he definitely doesn't fake high-tech mass destruction.

So I told them I'd fake it. Then I used the real stuff anyway.

All the cameras? Demolished. All the trailers? Obliterated. Mark-Paul Gosselaar? MIA. And the pissing Cupids? Pretty sure they pissed themselves in the split second before I incinerated them with my multi-warhead hypersonic missiles.

I had to pay for it all, which was fine, because I'm rich. And George Lukas was pretty pissed at me. Might've had something to do with the arm he lost, maybe. But it was all totally worth it. I had a hell of a good time. And guess what?

The few hours of footage they shot before I blew the shit out of everything ended up being the biggest hit in the history of Snapchat. Got a couple billion views. Won a dozen Webbys, whatever those are, plus five Emmys, all for special effects and hair and mustache styling. Got nominated for an Oscar but didn't win—which I count as a win because we weren't even a movie.

And just like that, same as in the rest of my life, I was a champion. A Hollywood megastar.

I got hired to star in the new(est) *Knight Rider* movie for this smash-hit new platform called Quibi. Bankrupted the whole operation when I blew up their entire fleet of advanced, talking AI Lamborghini Huracáns on the very first day.

I mean, what did they expect? Everyone knows I only drive black. So what if they were billion-dollar cars with next-gen 6G quantum-computing techno-brains that may have qualified as sentient beings and/or taken over the world like Skynet in *The Terminator.* They were all fucking red. They deserved to be eviscerated!

Then I got cast in—and became the only star in—*The Expendables 7: Rise of the Doc.* I say "the only star" because as soon as they found out I was gonna be in their little movie, Stallone, Schwarzenegger, and Statham all bailed because they knew I'd make 'em look like a bunch of skinny punks.

That one actually started out okay—it was gonna be this nice, sweet family film about the Expendables (me) overthrowing the democratically elected Nicaraguan government and installing an American puppet regime (also me). But then everyone got pissed when I really *did* overthrow the Nicaraguan government, not to mention Colombia's and Peru's, just for shits and giggles.

I'm not an unreasonable megastar, so I bought brand-new PlayStation 5s for the entire populace of each country, and that seemed to smooth things over for a sec. But then it went to shit all over again when I told the director he'd have to ditch the title *The Expendables*—because the Two-Time clearly is *irreplaceable.* Just wasn't believable, you know?

Anyway, both *Knight Rider: The Fall of Quibi* and *The Mustachables 7: Rise of the Doc* still ended up being huge blockbusters. The people want what they want, you know? And what the people want is *real* destruction, *real* dominance, *real* athleticism, *real* onyx-black mullets. Even if that means I have to bruise a few egos, bankrupt a few companies, and blow up a few small countries to get it done, all right? Because what the people *want* is Dr Disrespect.

I understood that, and soon the entertainment industry—or "the Biz of Show," as we insiders call it—did too.

I built myself a swanky new complex in the Hollywood Hills—to make room, I had to tear down Vin Diesel's mansion and Jet Li's and the Rock's, but none of them seemed to mind once they realized how much taller I am.

I was the main draw at all the red carpets. I hosted exclusive invitation-only *Call of Duty* battle royales at my pad with all the biggest A-list stars—Dolph Lundgren, Wesley Snipes, Billy Zane, Stephen Dorff, Michael Madsen, Jean-Claude Van Damme—and a couple times I even let Billy Zane almost win, just for fun. Hell, JCVD moved into my guesthouse and I didn't even know about it for five weeks—my estate is so damn huge I'd never even *seen* my guesthouse.

It was a fucking blast. For a while, anyway.

But it got stale real quick.

No matter how hard I tried, I couldn't get any of the red carpets changed to black. Which, I mean, unacceptable. Billy Zane got mad when he found out I was only letting him almost-win, and then he got *super* mad when I wouldn't hire him to play my chauffeur in *The Mustachables 9: Slick Daddy's Revenge.* And JCVD and Razor Frank did *not* get along. JCVD was a toilet-paper-under guy and Razor Frank was strictly toilet-paper-over. I mean, unforgivable.

JCVD is a tough guy and all, but they don't call him Razor Frank for nothing. Meaning he will *cut* your punk face with a razor blade if he doesn't like the way you hang your TP. I felt so bad for JCVD I gave him the chauffeur part.

You know that eye patch he wore in the film? Yeah, that wasn't done for dramatic effect. Jean-Claude Van Damme literally has no right eyeball anymore.

So yeah, just like with *Airwolf,* I grew up watching these guys. I thought they were all badasses. All right, I never really liked Stephen Dorff, but everyone else—badasses.

I mean, Dolph Lundgren alone. We're talking He-Man in *Masters of the Universe.* We're talking Drago in *Rocky IV.* We're talking the original Punisher of motion picture cinema. The man's got a jaw almost as square as mine. He's six feet five inches tall, so, you know, not as tall as me, but still pretty damn tall. And I don't know what kind of mousse he uses on his hair—fine, I asked, it's L'Oréal Studio Line with its patented Multi-Vitamin Formula for Protection and Shine—but those blond spikes are like indestructible nails of gold-plated solid gold.

Then, one day, we're all hanging out at my mega-mansion, eating Papa John's, pounding Pabst, and the dude farts.

Now, that, in and of itself, is cool, right? It's like, "Whoa, mega action icon Dolph Lundgren just farted in **my** house on **my** jet-black Corinthian-leather sectional sofa"—like, what a fucking honor, you know?

And I'm expecting like this awesome riiiiiip. Like a ragged, raging *chainsaw* of a fart that revs up and roars, leaving a path of devastation and destruction in its wake. Like, I'm ready to be *impressed*, man.

But guess what?

This guy lets out the weakest, whiniest, most pathetic fart I've heard in my life. In my life!!! It's this high-pitched, squeaky, mousy little paw just scratching at the screen door, pleading to be let in for a saucer of milk at suppertime.

The other guys there, Terry Crews and Jesse Ventura and Antonio Banderas and Kelsey Grammer, they all give each other this knowing look. Like, *Oh—it's one of Dolph's embarrassing weak-ass farts again.*

Then I look at Dolph, and he kind of shrugs and in his Swedish accent he goes, "Sorry, my bad."

And that was just it for me, you know?

Like, all right, so you've got a clinically weak fart. I mean, it's lame, it sucks, but whatever—it happens. But then to *apologize for it*???

NO.

Up on the big silver screen—or in syndicated television and various infomercials—these guys all seemed larger than life. They were men to be respected. To be admired. They were heroes! Almost—*almost*—as cool as me!

But in real life? They were average human beings who apologized for below-average farts.

I became disillusioned, to say the least. For the very first time in my life.

I'd accomplished everything I'd ever set out to accomplish. I'd climbed the highest mountains. I'd flown through the clouds and the smoke with the eagles. I'd hunted with the wolves and swum with the stingrays. I'd won every tournament, I'd beaten every challenge, I'd destroyed every so-called champion.

I'd had not just one origin story but three. I'd won the Blockbuster Video Game Championship—twice, in 1993 and 1994. I'd foiled the founders of Oogle, who turned out to be totally evil. I'd obliterated the world's oldest crime syndicate, then established my own league of warriors called the Champions Club. And I'd become the greatest, most authentic, most real Hollywood star of all time, single-handedly rebooting *Airwolf* and *Knight Rider* and even giving Jean-Claude Van Damme a place to live.

I'd dominated every step of the way. And they were big steps, because I have massive feet.

But now? What was there? What was left to challenge me?

Nothing, that's what.

Shit, I almost forgot. I guess Nigel the Editor did call me up and ask me to write a book to save literature. That was something. But now I've obviously done that too.

You're welcome, literature.

So the Two-Time has officially accomplished everything there is possible to accomplish on the face of this earth. It's time. Time to really retire.

Oh yeah. There is one more thing.

CHAPTER 14

WHAT I'M THE DOCTOR OF

Now, I know what you're thinking.

You're thinking, "Oh, Doc, of course the last thing you're gonna do is rescue Nigel the Editor from the evil clutches of the Brotherhood and save the day like the badass hero you are!"

As usual, you're completely wrong.

I would've been willing to overlook all his sloppiness, all his arrogance, all his "indeed"s and "forsooth"s and his other pseudointellectual BS. I would've forgiven the way he crapped on my "yayaya" world record and gave me shit about selling my high-class merch. I would've forgiven—but I wouldn't have forgotten, because the Doc *never forgets*.

But when Nigel the Editor quit my book, when he decided of his own free will to abandon Team Doc, he severed our bonds forever. I mean, I *told* the guy he might need my help someday—I told him!—way back on page whatever-it-was. And what did he do? He crapped a big steamy crap right on the face of everything we once shared, everything we once had.

And yeah, I know that metaphor is rough, but that's how strong I feel about this!

And I'm sorry—hahaha, not at all—but there's just no coming back from that, you know? Especially if "coming back" literally means I gotta fly a thousand miles in my chopper, battle hundreds of bloodthirsty knife-wielding henchmen, topple an ancient international criminal organization—*again*—and rescue your punk ass from a diabolical hunchback named Carl.

I mean, I haven't even had lunch today!

I'm finally on my very last leftover chicken fajita plate from that first meeting at App Lebeés. When was that—four months ago? Five? Really amazing how well that stuff keeps. Can't wait to dig in.

But because I'm a nice guy—seriously the nicest guy ever in existence—I have decided to honor Nigel the Editor's last request. Or what will stand as his last request once the Brotherhood, you know, murders him or whatever.

That's right. I'll finally reveal to you, to the world, and to the memory of Nigel the Editor himself what, exactly, I am a doctor of.

And it's all explained in my unprecedented, never-before-revealed fourth—that's right, fourth!—origin story. Which I will proceed to tell . . .

NOW!

———

This will be hard, maybe even impossible, for your mind to comprehend, but in Dimension Quark there was a time when the Doctor wasn't the Doctor.

That's right. This dimension happens to be named after the most fundamental particle of physics. A pillar of quantum mechanics. A cornerstone of the universe itself. It's a dimension in which time, space, and probability all combined to create the most profound, fundamental manifestation of reality ever envisioned by god or man: me.

So anyway, I was about ten and the fam and I were on a fun little vacay, right?

No big deal, just driving our brand-new Dodge Caravan around the country, stopping at campsites, seeing the sights.* To be honest, I straight-up had no idea where we'd been or where we were going, because I spent the whole time locked on my Game Boy, demolishing one *Tetris* world record after another.

Except for the video games, most of the time I was bored off my ass. I mean, camping? Really? I was a ten-year-old mini-champion in the making. Ready for new worlds to conquer, new foes to obliterate, new Lamborghinis to purchase and then crash in awesome high-speed chases. What the fuck did I care about roughing it?

Until we arrived at California's Mount Whitney, the biggest mountain in America.

And yeah, if you want to be a smart-ass you might be like, "But, Doc, isn't Mount McKinley in Alaska bigger?"

Then I'd laugh viciously and be like, "Everyone knows Alaska isn't *really* America. Also, shut up."

This mountain was the most incredible thing I'd ever seen in my life. And at ten years old, I'd been around. We're talking purple mountain majesty—WOW. We're talking jagged cliffs with sheer

---

* In this dimension, both my parents were grade-school teachers, and they had an irrational hatred for used-car dealers. There was no Razor Frank— no Razor Frank at all! Think about it.

drops of fourteen thousand feet—WOW. We're talking snowy crags and lethal pines and snarling rabid wolves howling into the infinite blue sky—**WOOOO-OOOOOOOOOWWWWW!**

I knew, right then and there, as I looked up from my Game Boy—this time dominating *Castlevania*, another pretty sick Game Boy adaptation—that I was going to climb that mountain. I was gonna make it all the way to the tippity-top. And I was going to do it alone.

I waited till later that night, when we'd all bunked down in our tent. My folks were snuggled into their matching goose-down sleeping bags, me in my He-Man sleeping bag, which didn't match a damn thing because I live life on my own terms, baby. They fell asleep at like 9:15, because they were lame and old, though I obviously loved them dearly because, you know, they did give birth to a man-god.

I looked one last time at my snoozing, snoring parents, turned to the fabric He-Man on my bedding, whispered, *"Keep an eye on 'em for me, buddy. I might not make it back,"* and escaped into the night.

My heart was pounding like the drum of a Celtic shaman. The stars shined brighter than the eyes of a cosmic eagle. The sky was the blackest black I'd ever seen. Blacker than coal, blacker than slate, blacker than the mood of my defeated enemies. Blacker even than my hair.

Just kidding, nothing is blacker than my hair.

I began my ascent. Even at a young age, I had the preternatural speed of a killer cheetah, so I moved quickly, confidently, never tiring, barely breaking a sweat, and always smelling great.

I could hear the animals of the ancient wilderness all around me. The guttural growls of the mountain lions. The subtle slitherings of the snake. The ghostly hoots of the owls. But none of them felt threatening to me. Instead, they seemed like kindred spirits. My wild warrior family. A source of additional strength and ferocity as I climbed higher and higher, hour after hour.

The air grew colder, thinner, and although my young skin was already thick and tough and leathery, I started to wish I'd changed into something warmer than my Spider-Man PJs. I was up so high I could see the clouds all around me, reflected in the moonlight. The mists, the winds, and the clouds swirled everywhere. Eagles soared past me, screaming in fury and brotherly awe at my boldness—it felt like I was flying with them, at a whole new level of greatness.

Time ticked by, and on I climbed. The lack of oxygen became like fire in my throat. I could sense my normally catlike vision starting to blur. My calves, usually so supple and springy, were growing slack. My glutes, usually so chiseled and firm, were becoming soft and spongy. My five-foot-four frame, usually so powerful, was beginning to wilt.

Shit, this mountain-climbing thing was tougher than I'd imagined.

Then, just as I thought it would never end, just when I almost— *almost*—began to know fear for the first time in my young life, I was there.

At the Top of the Mountain.

My energy returned to me in a rush, my power crashing through me like oceanic waves. I raised my fists in the air, tossed back my flowing masculine mullet, and shouted into the heavens with my brothers the coyotes:

YAYAYAYA!

And then, from behind me, I heard a whisper, like a rustling of leaves on the jungle floor.

"Ah, so you're here."

I turned and saw a grizzled old man, his back stooped with the passage of time, his twisted gray beard hanging down to his waist. He had a big-ass mole right above his left eye. It was disgusting, and the more I tried not to look at it, the more I looked at it.

"Who are you?" I asked.

"I've been waiting for you for many a year, child."

"Yeah," I said. "All this speaking in mysterious riddles? Super annoying."

"Ah," he chuckled. "The prophecy said you would be a bit of an asshole but in a funny kind of way. Let's hope at least the second part is also true."

Now I was really getting pissed. I was more than funny—I was hilarious!

"Look, man," I said. "I don't care how old you are or how tired I am—you better start giving me answers or I'm gonna have to beat your weird mystic hermit ass."

He sat down on this little boulder with a groan.

"Well," he said, "you pretty much just said it. I'm a weird mystic hermit. And I've been waiting here forever. Or about five or six years, give or take. All because of a dream I had. A dream that someday a boy would walk up this lonely mountain in the middle of the night. A boy of exceptional athleticism, unsurpassed skill, and otherworldly hair. A boy who would go on to be the greatest online gaming champion the world had ever known.

"And I—I was to give this boy a message. And a name."

"A name?" I asked.

"Yes," he said. "The name-ame-ame is Doctor-octor-octor Disrespect-ect-ect-ect."

And when he said it, there *really was* this awesome badass reverb!

I swear the dude didn't move his lips funny or do anything strange with his mouth or anything. It was just this amazing reverb effect. It electrified the air and shook the very cliffs on which we stood.

I've been trying to replicate it ever since.

Then I asked the first question that pretty much anyone would've asked.

"I'm ten years old. What am I a doctor of?"

"It's an acronym," he said. "Obviously."

"Oh, right!" I laughed. Then I got super serious: "Dude, did you not just hear me? I'm ten years old. I have no idea what an acronym is."

"Simple," he said gravely. "Each letter of 'Doctor' stands for a different powerful component of your uniquely awesome character."

"Ohhhh," I said. "So you're ripping off 'Shazam'?"

"Shut up," he said. "Anyway, here's how it breaks down. The 'D' stands for 'deadly.' Because you're a master of destruction.

" 'O' stands for 'omnipotent.' Because you are as close to all-powerful as a mortal man can be without being divine.

" 'C' stands for 'crazy.' Because I think we can all agree that you're pretty damn crazy.

" 'T' stands for 'Titan.' Because your massive, powerful, athletic frame will allow you to dominate all who challenge you.

"That brings us to the next 'O,' " he said. "For 'omniscient.' Because you will be wise and all-knowing.

"And finally there's 'R,' which stands for 'rage,' " he said. "Because you are one angry son of a bitch."

I smiled. Because sure, he was right about the whole rage thing—he was right about everything—but I also have one hell of a good-looking smile.

"And what about 'Disrespect'?" I asked. "What does that stand for?"

"Doesn't stand for anything. You're just a bit of an asshole," he said.

I thought about the name. Was "Dr Disrespect" the moniker, the identity, I wanted to embrace for the rest of my life? I mean, yeah, the gnarly old hermit dude seemed cool enough—definitely a BO issue, and that big mole was like a car wreck, but everything he'd said had been spot-on. Yet this was a huge decision. One that would impact my future, shape my destiny. It would have implications not just for me, but for every enemy I obliterated, every civilization I crushed, every world I dominated.

Took me about a second to make up my mind.

"The name-ame-ame is Doctor-octor-octor Disrespect-ect-ect-ect."

Saying my new name felt right. It felt good. It felt . . . "me."

The hermit guy said, "You know I can see your lips moving when you make that reverb sound, right?"

"DAMN IT!" I said. "HOW DID YOU MAKE THAT COOL SOUND?"

"You'll figure it out," he chuckled. "Someday."

"'Someday'? Well, that's super annoying—thanks for nothing, hermit guy."

And, completely justified in my anger, I turned to go.

"Wait!" he shouted.

"Look, dude," I said. "Maybe you could, like, tell me what to do before. But things have changed now that I'm the Doc. The Doc don't take orders from no man."

"There's one more thing," he said. "A message I have to give you before you leave."

"Chop-chop," I said. "I still gotta get down this mountain, and if I know my mom I got a bowl of Mr. T cereal waiting there for me right now."

He looked into my eyes. He was graver, more solemn, than I'd ever seen him. And seriously, it took every ounce of my will not to grab that damn mole and try to twist it off.

"Even with all your powers," he said. "Even with all your strength and cunning. Even with your domination of every arena known to man, you will have one weakness, Dr Disrespect."

"Lies!"

"And that weakness is your unquenchable thirst for challenge. Your unstoppable need for competition. Because no matter how successful you are, no matter how dominant, no matter how high you climb, it will never be enough. You will always want more."

"NO!" I shouted. "IT'S IMPOSSIBLE! I'M THE DOC! **I HAVE NO WEAKNESSES!**"

"Really?" He smiled. "Where are you now?"

"I'm at the top," I said. "I'm at the tippity-top of the mountain!"

"Then what, my friend, is that?"

He pointed above us. I looked, and I couldn't believe my eyes.

I was at the top of the mountain. And I was still only halfway up.

———

FUCK.

Man, I'm so sorry, you guys. I mean, I know we pretty much reached a natural ending point to that incredible moment in Doc lore, but still—I wanted a few beats to savor it, you know? To really bask in the powerful emotional impact.

But yeah, I got this urgent message from Nigel the Editor's AIM account.

So this right here is an official . . .

Real-Time Update

And of course we all know that this isn't Nigel the Editor contacting me anymore. This is Carl the Hunchback.

I thought you said you were going to delete AOL Instant Messenger, Doc.

Whatever, man. I've been busy telling amazing stories here, but I'll delete it this afternoon.

I'm happy you still have it now. It'll give you a chance to see your old friend Nigel the Editor in his last few extremely painful moments.

What—AIM has video? No way!

Well, we had to add that functionality ourselves.

Shit, I guess you Brotherhood punks are good at something—OUCH, that does not look like fun for Nigel the Editor. What is that—a buzz saw slowly moving toward his nuts?

Yes.

And tweezers yanking out his nose hairs one by one?

Uh-huh.

And clamps twisting his nipples into little knots?

He actually requested that.

Yeah, I don't need to know. Anyway, guess I'll let you guys get back to it—

"DOC, PLEASE! SAVE ME! PLEEEEEASE!"

Ah shit, do you really have to scream so loud, Nigel the Editor?

"YES!"

WOW! Is that a portable 7T-43 laser-induced plasma-effect weapon with sonic boosters? I thought I was the only person who had one of those! I've never actually seen it vibrate anyone's brain before.

"PLEASE, I'M BEGGING YOU!"

Ah shit, man. I mean, I would, but—I haven't even finished my lunch yet. Wanna see the explanation about what I'm a doctor of that I wrote for you? Maybe I can email it and the Brotherhood can let you read it or something.

"I CAN'T READ! MY EYEBALLS ARE FULL OF ACID!! AHHHHHHHHHHHHHHHHHHHHHHHHHHHHHHHHHHHHHH-HHHHHH!"

Sigh.

"AAAAAAAAAHHHHHHHHHHHHHHHHHHHHHHHHH-HHHHHHHHHHHHHHHHHHHHHHHHHHHHHHHHHHHHHH-HHHHHHHHHHHHHHHHHHHHHHHHHHHHHHHHHHHHHH-HHHHHHHHHHHHHHHHHHHHHHHHHHHHHHHHHHHHHH-HHHHHHHHHHHHHHHHHHHHHHHHHHHHHHHHHHHHHH-HHHHHHHHHHHHHHHHHHHHHHHHHHHHHHHHHHHHHH-HHHHHHHHHHHHHHHHHHHHHHHHHHHHHHHHHHHHHH-HHHHHHHHHHHHHH!"

All right, all right, I get it! Dude, chill out! I'll rescue you, all right? Fuck! I could've told you like ten minutes ago if you'd just stop screaming like a skinny little punk!

Honestly, between me and you, I was always gonna do it. I just wanted to make you sweat it out a little, you know? Look, I'm still a little pissed that you walked off my book. And if I'm being honest here, I just think you could work on your people skills, you know? I mean, I'm the talent. I'm the Doc. And I expect to be treated with a certain degree of respect.

"AAAAAAAAAAAAAAAAAAAAAAAAAAAAAAAAAAAAAA-
AAAAHHHHHHHHHHHHHHHHHHHHHHHHHHHHHHH-
HHHHHHHHHHHHHHHHHHHHHHHHHHHHHHHHHHH-
HHHHHHHHHHHHHHHHHHHHHHHHHHHHHHHHHHH-
HHHHHHHHHHHHHHHHHHHHHHHHHHHHHHHHHHH-
HHHHHHHHHHHHHHHHHHHHHHHHHHHHHHHHHHH-
HHHHHHHHHHHHHHHHHHHHHHHHHHHHHHHHHHH-
HHHHHHHHHHHHHHHHHHHHHHHHHHHHHHHHHHH-
HHHHHHHHHHHHHHHHHHHHHHHHHHHHHHHHHHH-
HHHHHHHHHHHHHHHHHHHHHHHHHHHHHHHHHHH-
HHHHHHHHHHHHHHHHHHHHHHHHHHHHHHHHHHH-
HHHHHHHHHHHHHHHHHHHHHHHHHHHHHHHHHHH-
HHHHHHHHHHHHHHHHHHHHHHHHHHHHHHHHHHH-
HHHHHHHHHHHHHHHHHHHHHHHHHHHHHHHHHHH-
HHHHHHHHHHHHHHHHHHHHHHHHHHHHHHHHHHH-
HHHHHHHHHHHHHHHHHHHHHHHHHHHHHHHHHHH-
HHHHHHHHHHHHHHHHHHHHHHHHHHHHHHHHHHH-
HHHHHHHHHHHHHHHHHHHHHHHHHHHHHHHHHHH-
HHHHHHHHHHHHHHHHHHHHHHHHHHHHHHHHHHH-
HHHHHHHHHHHHHHHHHHHHHHHHHHHHHHHHHHH-
HHHHHHHHHHHHHHHHHHHHHHHHHHHHHHHHHHH-
HHHHHHHHHHHHHHHHHHHHHHHHHHHHHHHHHHH-
HHHHHHHHHHHHHHHHHHHHHHHHHHHHHHHHHHH-
HHHHHHHHHHHHHHHHHHHHHHHHHHHHHHHHHHH-

HHHHHHHHHHHHHHHHHHHHHHHHHHHHHHHHHHHH-
HHHHHHHHHHHHHHHHHHHHHHHHHHHHHHHHHHHH-
HHHHHHHHHHHHHHHHHHHHHHHHHHHHHHHHHHHH-
HHHHHHHHHHHHHHHHHHHHHHHHHHHHHHHHHHHH-
HHHHHHHHHHHHHH!"

But anyway, you messed up, I think you understand that now, I'm sure you won't do it again, and I'm willing to let bygones be bygones. I'm happy to be the bigger man here. Because when it's all said and done, I still love you, man. I still appreciate everything you've done for me and for the book and for the entire Champions Club. And I really am the bigger man out of the two of us, like a lot bigger, both literally and figuratively, and I think the facts back that up.

All right, cool. So I'm gonna finish up this chicken fajita, then I might need a nap. And then, when I'm good and ready, I'll come rescue you from the Brotherhood. Cool?

Oh hey, Carl the Hunchback—where am I meeting you guys to kick your ass? Hong Kong again? You got a new lame-ass warehouse for me to demolish?

I'm glad you asked, Doc. The setting will be a bit . . . different this time.

Whoa whoa whoa whoa whoa. What are you showing me right now, bro? I thought you were inside, but that looks like gleaming silvery skyscrapers. Like shining spotlights and flashing bulbs and paparazzi and international press with TV cameras and helicopters and Lamborghinis and A-list stars and plush red carpets and all the glitzy glamour of a MAJOR EXCLUSIVE INVITATION-ONLY GLOBAL PAY-PER-VIEW GALA EVENT. That's my kind of torture chamber, baby!

That's right, Doc. I know you like . . . attention. We're holding Nigel the Editor at the very top of the world's tallest building in the heart of Dubai. And we invited the world's top press, the galaxy's biggest stars, and the most powerful, influential people in the cosmos to witness our final showdown. We'll be waiting.

I disconnected AIM and arched one of my perfectly sculpted slate-black eyebrows.

A life-and-death rescue mission on the world's tallest building in Dubai in front of the eyes and cameras of the entire sentient universe?

This just got interesting.

CHAPTER 15

THE END???

So I'm flying my Ka-27 attack chopper through the clear Dubai night sky, dictating directly to my advanced prototype Casio TP-4000X microcassette recorder.

As usual, I know exactly what you're thinking: "Doc, why are you dictating? Why not just wait to type this up later on your experimental Dell Inspiron with WordPerfect 5.1 emulator?"

As usual, I'm nice enough to answer your impertinent questions. And the simple fact is that even though I'm the most dominant champion in the history of mankind, when you live a life like mine, a life that's always on the edge, a life that's always at the tippity-top of the mountain and only halfway up—there's risk. There's danger. There's a chance I might not make it home.

If there wasn't, it wouldn't be a challenge. And I wouldn't be the Doc.

My copter is getting closer to the tallest building in the world. And I gotta admit—that thing is really tall. Like, you know how sometimes people are like, "Wow, that building is tall," and you see it, and you're like, "Yeah, that building is tall—but with my six-foot-eight frame and my superior athleticism, I bet I could still jump it"?

Well, this building isn't like that.

I see it standing alone and unchallenged on the Dubai skyline, like a dagger plunging blindly into the black heart of night. Shit, that was poetic. I fly closer, and I see klieg lights sweeping across the heavens, with dozens of other, less cool helicopters circling the top, trying desperately to get a glimpse of the action.

I cut right through the crowd, because the Two-Time always cuts through the crowd, and my Kamov pulls in close for a perfect landing.

Just before I touch down, I scan the crowds, and for once in his pathetic life Carl the Hunchback wasn't lying. Everyone is there. Everyone!

All the TV press that's been covering me, drooling over me since I won my first Blockbuster Championship—Tom Brokaw and Dan Rather and my old buddy Wolf Blitzer and some dude I don't recognize from ABC because who the fuck can really replace Peter Jennings? And next to them all the A-list stars and champions I've encountered throughout my life—Leo and Brad and Fred Savage and JCVD and the ShamWow guy and Just Plain Usman and Kangaroo Jack Hortly and even Dolph Lundgren, who really is a good dude even if his farts are weak. And then the most powerful executives in the universe—there's Mr. Blockbuster, and Sergey and Larry from Oogle, and of course Zuck and Bill and Bezos, who I just closed a $10 billion deal with on my flip phone on the flight here. And there—there are my parents! And I do a double take, because there are six of them from various different dimensions!

And they all look mostly identical, except, like, one of my dads has brown eyes, and another has green eyes, and another has one brown eye and one green eye, and cool little interdimensional differences like that. And there are at least seven Razor Franks, and who even knows what the fuck languages they all speak.

And I land my Kamov on my reserved helipad, and I open the cockpit and flashes are going off and TV cameras are rolling and the crowds are cheering and I step onto the plush red carpet and I flick my flowing requiem-black mullet back over my shoulder in this really slick way.

And speaking of slick, a lifetime supply of **SLICK, BY DOC** is still available NOW at InterdimensionalChampionsClub.gg for the ridiculously awesome price of $1,399.99.

And then Bell Biv DeVoe and Lionel Richie start harmonizing my awesome theme song live for the entire crowd to hear:

Bump-tsshhh.

Bump-tsshhh-tsshhh.

"They call him Doc!"

Oh fucking yeah. All the great influences are here from my past. Everyone I've respected. Everyone I've loved. Everyone I've beaten—and that's everyone. If I didn't have an icebox where my heart used to be, that heart would be warmed.

Now I'm seeing Carl the Hunchback, and he's wearing a little hunchback tuxedo—honestly, a classy touch—and he's surrounded by heavily armed guards and standing next to Nigel the Editor, who's strapped down on a stainless-steel table with a buzz saw headed toward his nuts.

I look around, and I smile my sly, cunning smile, and I hold up my massive hands, and I shout:

"ENOUGH!"

Suddenly there's silence.

"Welcome, Dr Disrespect," Carl the Hunchback says, "to the ultimate challenge of your life."

"AHHHHHHHHHHHHHHHHHHHHHHHHHHHHHHHHHH-HHHH!" Nigel the Editor screams.

"I'm up for any challenge you or the Brotherhood has for me," I say. "And I gotta admit—even I'm impressed by the badass setup. You guys must have an amazing event planner. But before this goes any further, don't you think we should end your little charade?"

"What charade?" Carl the Hunchback asks.

Hahaha, like I'm gonna fall for his bullshit.

"You know," Carl the Hunchback says, "we can hear everything you're saying into your tape recorder. And my question wasn't bullshit."

I shout, "You know exactly the charade I'm talking about. It's the final twist ending you've set up since the beginning of this book—and I've seen it coming a mile away."

Carl the Hunchback and Nigel the Editor kinda look at each other.

"The two of you," I say, "are really . . . the SAME PERSON."

"Uhhh," they reply.

"That's right! Nigel the Editor is really Carl the Hunchback, and there was no kidnapping or torture at all!"

"But . . . ," Carl the Hunchback says, "but we're both right here. Right in front of you. Right now."

I laugh. "You can't fool me. All of it—writing my book and saving literature and treating me to lunch at App Lebeés—it was all just an elaborate ploy so the Brotherhood could get its final diabolical revenge!"

"Doc," Nigel the Editor says, "I know we've had our differences, but you're totally embarrassing yourself right now. And this saw is almost shaving the fuzz off my peaches."

I scratch my insanely square chin. "So . . . Simon & Schuster really is paying me to write a book?"

"Indeed."

"And, Carl the Hunchback, you're absolutely, positively *sure* that's really—"

"YES, IT'S A REAL FUCKING HUNCHBACK," he screams. "THE DOCTORS CAN'T DO A THING ABOUT IT, I'M HIGHLY SENSITIVE ABOUT MY APPEARANCE, AND CAN WE PLEASE JUST MOVE ON TO MY ULTIMATE VENGEANCE?!"

"Fine," I say. "But only because I say so."

Carl the Hunchback takes a deep breath. And it's like, learn to regulate your emotions, you know? You're supposed to be the head of a major international criminal—

"I can still hear your dictation, Doc. But more important, I've invited all these people here today to bear witness. It is well-known that you're the greatest competitor the world has ever seen. Mostly because you never let us forget it. You've won every battle, you've dominated every challenge. Your athleticism is unparalleled, and your silky hair is the only thing blacker than your soul. Your mustache is registered as a lethal weapon in twenty-three countries. You crave combat. You live for danger. You *lust* after battle."

"Hey, keep it PG-13 for the kids, man."

"But," he says, "what happens when you finally meet your match? What happens when you finally face a challenge you can't overcome? What happens when, for the very first time in your life, you finally lo—"

"DON'T EVEN FINISH THAT SENTENCE!" I shout. "IT'LL NEVER HAPPEN! THE DOC WILL NEVER, EVER LOSE!"

Then I hear this, like, awkward coughing noise, and I look out into the crowd, and—holy shit, it's Sensei Billy with his nasty pubey goatee!

"Um," he says, "I'm pretty sure I got you once back in the eighties . . ."

"THAT WAS BEST-TWO-OUT-OF-THREE," I yell. "AND I HAD NOT YET CLAIMED THE SACRED MANTLE OF THE DOC! GET YOUR FUCKING LORE STRAIGHT, BILL!"

"Whatever. I'm just here for the vol-au-vents."

"I repeat," I snarl, loud enough for the world to hear me even without the mics of every major news organization shoved into my face, "I. WILL. NEVER. LOSE."

Carl the Hunchback laughs. I gotta give the guy credit—it's a pretty solid evil laugh. He's totally been working on it.

"I'm glad you made that perfectly clear, Doc," he says. "Because in order to save your friend Nigel here, you won't have to kill anyone. You won't have to shoot anyone. You won't even have to stab anyone."

"Seriously?" I say. "This is starting to sound dull."

"No, you will simply have to play—and win—a new video game. A game we ordered developed by the greatest gaming minds of all time, everyone from Midway to Nintendo to Riot to Epic. A game that combines the gore of *Mortal Kombat* with the gameplay of *Halo*. The power of *Call of Duty* with the totally inexplicable popularity of *Fortnite*. The ingenuity of *Apex Legends* with the iconic status of *Mike Tyson's Punch-Out!!* And yes, Mike Tyson is in it, and yes, he bites off someone's ear.

"It is quite simply the grandest of all the grand games the universe has ever known."

"Uh-huh," I say. "I'll be the judge of that."

"And you'll have to compete against the latest, super-advanced, high-performance, perfectly perfected version of the only opponent you've ever struggled against: Lord Hannn."

The platform that Nigel the Editor is being tortured on slides to the side and he screams in terror, except no one really cares because the shit that's revealed is fucking awesome.

A massive 146-inch 6K experimental Sony Trinitron plasma flat-screen TV with a Bose sound system the size of a semitruck. Holy fuck, do I love a good subwoofer! And connected to that is an advanced prototype PS7 that for no good reason is plated in twenty-four-karat gold and encrusted with diamonds and fine furs. And connected to that is a brand-spanking-new Lord Hannn robot. And this robot is like the Borg hive queen meets the ED-209 meets Number Five Is Alive meets the original Terminator with all his skin fried off. We're talking polished black steel, we're talking motherboards and wires and flashing lights, we're talking human brains floating in vats of pink goo hooked up to tubes and blue lightning bolts randomly shooting from one electrode to another and smoke and steampunk dials and gears and AI and graphic equalizers, and I'm pretty sure I saw a flux capacitor somewhere in there too. Also? No Xbox-controller hand.

"All right, that does look cool," I say. "But 'struggled' is a total stretch."

"So, Dr Disrespect," Carl the Hunchback says. "Do you accept this challenge?"

I look at what's unquestionably the most advanced experimental computer in the cosmos, the greatest opponent anyone has ever faced. I look at Nigel the Editor, sobbing for his life. I look at the cameras, the press, the celebrities, hanging on my every word, waiting for my next move.

I think about all the adversity I've faced in my life. All the struggles. All the obstacles I've overcome. I think about all the times I've stared down the long, dark alleyways of fear. All the times I could've chosen to stay in the sunlight or hide with the crowds. All the times I pressed on despite the odds and just *barely* snatched death from the hungry jaws of life.

And I laugh, long and loud. Because was there ever really a question?

"Bring it on," I growl.

My audience—the entire world!—roars its approval.

I walk over to the platform. Along the way I offer firm handshakes to a few of the onlookers—Fred Savage, Killer Commie Ivan, and, sure, even Stephen Dorff—because they are, after all, a part of my story, and that makes them lucky bastards.

I pause at my old comrade in fine literature, Nigel the Editor, still chained to the torture table, and I place my prototype Casio microcassette recorder in his weak hand.

"Take this," I whisper. "Finish my book. And don't forget—it was all worth it."

I pick up the controller and take my position across from my component opponent. I look at him, eye to laser sensor. And the game begins.

Carl the Hunchback was right. It really is the grandest of all games ever created in the universe. And I know, because I've won them all.

The Violence. The Speed. The Momentum. Absolutely unparalleled. Like nothing I've ever experienced. This is truly the single challenge worthy of the Doc. The tallest peak of the tallest mountain in the universe, and there is no halfway up.

I fight harder than I've ever fought before. I give it everything I have and more. I move faster, I react quicker, I destroy with more precision and anger and energy. I leave nothing behind.

As I battle—tirelessly, furiously, desperately—I can sense something changing around me. The atmosphere is growing thicker, more charged. Clouds begin to gather not just above us but *around* us, black and purple and full of fury.

People are pointing at the sky, gazing in wonder, murmuring and afraid. Kangaroo Jack says something like, "That's one baby-eating dingo!" and I chuckle. Good ol' Kangaroo Jack.

The mists are swirling faster and faster in a crazy mess of angry electric chaos. The moon is blotted out, the stars nowhere to be seen. A deep bellowing thunder rumbles across the land, and I feel the very foundations of the building tremble. Giant eagles soar through the night, circling around, and I swear they're screaming my name, calling to me over and over.

"DOC! DOOOCCCCCCC! DOOOOOOOCCCCCCCCCCC!"

Is there smoke? You're goddamn right there's smoke. And it's everywhere.

My artificial opponent is bursting with energy. His circuits are sparking and steaming, his sensors flashing blood red. He's the one being in the galaxy that can possibly match my skill, and he's closing in on his very first kill, the only kill that matters: me.

I feel myself slipping. For the first time in my legendary existence, I know that victory is falling out of my grasp.

It's a strange feeling. Is this what normal people go through every day? How can their average bodies bear it?

Maybe losing has always been inevitable because of who I am. If you're always hungry for a new challenge, if you're always hunting for more, if you refuse to be satisfied with being the best, maybe someday you simply *have to fail* no matter how good, how perfect, you are. After all, without real risk, is there really reward? Without loss, does winning truly mean a thing? Maybe I'd grow stronger if I finally came to terms with my own mortality, my own humanity. Maybe, just maybe, in the never-ending circle of life, this was all meant to be.

Hahahahaha. Yeah right.

I'm Dr Disrespect. And I'm gonna win this thing.

I eye the life meter on my screen. My power level is shrinking, on the brink of doom, absorbing blow after blow after blow.

150.

140.

Clouds churning, electricity crackling!

110.

95.

FUCK!

75.

55.

Buildings shaking, grown men weeping!

40.

30.

DAMN IT, COME ON, DOC!

10.

5.

Worlds colliding, dimensions bursting!

4.

3.

2.

RARRRRRRGGGGGGGGGGGGGGGH!

And then it happens.

One split second before I finally lose, one atomic instant before I, the Two-Time, the most dominant gaming superstar ever, experience failure for the very first time, a single bolt of lightning crashes down from the sky.

It slices through the air, cuts through the black of night, and strikes me. Electrifies every athletic molecule, ignites every devastating follicle, and irradiates the essence of my being.

And just like that, the Doc disappears. Vanishes.

Never to be seen again.

FROM THE DESK OF
NIGEL P. FARNSWORTH III

Greetings and salutations. My name is Nigel P. Farnsworth III, though I am perhaps best known to the readers of this memoir by the jocular sobriquet "Nigel the Editor."

Indeed I am the editor of this intriguing, rather—dare I say—unique entry into the canon of Western nonfiction. And I am here to attest, as an impartial observer of the action herein described, that it is, indeed, a work entirely of nonfiction.

Perhaps I do indeed say "indeed" too often, and Doc and I did indeed have our, shall we say, issues. But everything he says here is true in the most Platonic sense of the word, and I should know, because I studied classical philosophy at Brown.

Dr Disrespect really was struck by a bolt of lightning, after which he mysteriously vanished off the face of this earth, never to be seen again. We'll probably never know the real reason why. Perhaps the very concept of his losing was so anathema that the gods themselves decided to snatch him back to Mount Olympus. Perhaps his indomitable spirit simply soared to another, newer challenge on a higher cosmic plane, far from this world. Maybe he's just plain dead. Whatever it is, I count myself truly fortunate to have witnessed such an act of courage, power, and competitive passion, even if it came too late to save my lower-hanging testicle of the two.

Moments later, an elite commando squad from Doc's Champions Club took control of the area, arresting members of the Brotherhood, destroying what remained of the advanced AI Lord Hannn robot after the mysterious lightning bolt from the sky fried his circuits. Carl the Hunchback plummeted to his doom—again— and I am completely, absolutely, and sincerely convinced that this one will take and we will never ever see him again.

Thanks to Doc's more or less timely intervention, I was able to escape with nothing more injurious than permanent PTSD, fourth-degree burns over 70 percent of my body, a scar in the shape of someone "flipping the bird" that covers the entire right side of my face, a limp that permits me only to walk in rectangles, and my higher-hanging testicle of the two still completely intact.

As soon as I could leave my hospital bed, which only took three years, seven months, and twenty-two days, I took Doc's finished manuscript straight to Simon Schuster, the head of Simon & Schuster (the "&" is his middle initial). I slammed it on his desk and demanded that we publish immediately.

Yes, the book had already cost us millions in damages, and yes, the tallest building in the world had been razed to the ground, and yes, the democratically elected governments of several small nations and principalities had been overthrown. But in the process, hadn't we borne witness to the greatest feats of gaming and athleticism mankind has ever known? Hadn't we gained valuable tips on how to jump vertically, how to illegally drive a Lamborghini for a day, and how to comb a mullet with a switchblade comb safely? Hadn't we been a part of *history itself* when we observed in real time an actual flesh-and-blood man evaporate into the cosmic ether without a trace, never to be seen again?

Indeed, to quote the Doc himself, it was worth it.

Well, my friends, the book that's in front of you right now is evidence enough that Mr. Schuster agreed enthusiastically.

Of course, it probably didn't hurt that, thanks to Doc's mysterious disappearance, we didn't have to pay him a penny of the millions we contractually owed him. And that 2021 Lamborghini Aventador SVJ we bought for him? Needless to say, we *certainly* didn't have it repainted from red to black. I think we can all agree that cherry red is a far more festive color than dreary old black. Bleh!

In fact, as a small bonus for my troubles I even managed to convince Mr. Schuster to let me have Doc's Aventador all for myself. It looks so *perfect* in my garage right next to my Hummel collection—

Wait. Did you hear that?

A strange sound from outside my window. I'm sure it's nothing. But wait—there it is again.

Here, I'll just move aside my tweed curtain so I can see outside. *STOP! Who's there? Whoever's out there, I'm warning you! When I get angry I write very scathing letters!*

Dear God! Something in the distance, coming closer! Look at the size of that frame, so powerful! So athletic! And that mane of hair so black it is negative space against night itself! How quickly it moves toward my window, how decisively, how dominantly. Thank goodness I'm three stories up, no one can vertical-leap this high!

No! How—?!? It can't be! I saw you disappear! I—

DID YOU REALLY THINK I'D GIVE THAT PUNK EDITOR THE LAST WORD IN *MY* BOOK???

Oh, and the last word is . . .

YAYAYAYA!